CROCK·POT
• THE ORIGINAL SLOW COOKER •

100 top-rated RECIPES

pil

Publications International, Ltd.

Louis Weber, CEO
Publications International, Ltd.
7373 North Cicero Avenue
Lincolnwood, IL 60712

The recipes in this publication were developed for a medium-sized Crock-Pot® slow cooker unless specified otherwise in the recipe.

Photography on pages 7, 29, 31, 35, 47, 49, 51, 61, 73, 91, 99, 107, 115, 119, 131, 135, 139, 153, 161 and 171 PIL Photo Studio, Chicago.
Photographer: Jessica Dixon
Photographer's Assistant: Lauren Kessler
Food Stylists: Josephine Orba, Carol Smoler
Assistant Food Stylist: Lisa Dumstorff, Lissa Levy

Pictured on the front cover (clockwise from top): Pork Loin with Sherry and Red Onions *(page 138),* Wild Mushroom Beef Stew *(page 98),* Italian-Style Pot Roast *(page 152)* and Asian Sugar Snap Pea Soup *(page 114).*
Pictured on the back cover (clockwise from top): Vegetarian Chili *(page 36),* Black Bean Stuffed Peppers *(page 58),* Beef Stew *(page 122)* and Five-Spice Apple Crisp *(page 178).*

ISBN-13: 978-1-4508-4644-8
ISBN-10: 1-4508-4644-0

Library of Congress Control Number: 2012930245

Manufactured in China.

8 7 6 5 4 3 2 1

Table of Contents

How to get the best results from your CROCK-POT® slow cooker

To get the most from your **CROCK-POT®** slow cooker, keep the following hints and tips in mind.

Adding Ingredients at the End of the Cooking Time

Certain ingredients are best added toward the end of the cooking time. These include:

- **Milk, sour cream, and yogurt:** Add during the last 15 minutes.
- **Seafood and fish:** Add during the last 15 to 30 minutes.
- **Fresh herbs:** Fresh herbs such as basil will darken with long cooking, so if you want colorful fresh herbs, add them during the last 15 minutes of cooking or directly to the dish just before serving it.

Pasta and Rice

Converted rice holds up best through slow cooking. If the rice doesn't seem completely cooked after the suggested time, add an extra ½ cup to 1 cup of liquid per cup of rice, and extend the cooking time by 30 to 60 minutes.

Cooking Temperatures and Food Safety

According to the U.S. Department of Agriculture, bacteria in food is killed at a temperature of 165°F. As a result, it's important to follow the recommended cooking times and to keep the cover on your **CROCK-POT®** slow cooker during the cooking process to maintain food-safe temperatures. Slow-cooked meats and poultry are best when simmered gently for the period of time that allows the connective tissues to break down, yielding meat that is fall-off-the-bone tender and juicy.

Browning Meat

Meat will not brown as it would if it were cooked in a skillet or oven at a high temperature. It's not necessary to brown meat before slow cooking. However, if you prefer the look and flavor of browned meat, just brown it in a large skillet coated with oil, butter, or nonstick cooking spray, then place the browned ingredients into the stoneware and follow the recipe as written.

Herbs and Spices

When cooking with your **CROCK-POT®** slow cooker, use dried and ground herbs and spices, which work well during long cook times. However, the flavor and aroma of crushed or ground herbs may differ depending on their shelf life, and their flavor can lessen during the extended cooking time in the **CROCK-POT®** slow cooker.

Cooking for Larger Quantity Yields

Follow these guidelines to make a bigger batch in a larger unit, such as a 5-, 6-, or 7-quart **CROCK-POT®** slow cooker:

• Roasted meats, chicken, and turkey quantities may be doubled or tripled, and seasonings adjusted by half. *Caution:* Flavorful dried spices such as garlic or chili powder will intensify during long, slow cooking. Add just 25 to 50 percent more spices, as needed, to balance the flavors.

• When preparing a soup or a stew, you may double all ingredients except the liquids, seasonings, and dried herbs. Increase liquid volume by half, or adjust as needed.

• To avoid over or undercooking, always fill the stoneware ½ to ¾ full and conform to the recommended cook times (unless instructed otherwise by our **CROCK-POT®** slow cooker recipes).

• Do not double thickeners, such as cornstarch, at the beginning. You may always add more thickener later if it's necessary.

Cooking with Frozen Foods

Slow cooking frozen foods requires a longer cook time than fresh foods because the food needs more time to come up to safe internal temperatures. Meats also will require additional time to allow them to become tender. If there is any question about the cooking time, use a thermometer to ensure meats are cooking appropriately.

Removable Stoneware

The removable stoneware in your **CROCK-POT®** slow cooker makes cleaning easy. However, the stoneware insert can be damaged by sudden changes in temperature. Here are tips on the use and care of your stoneware:

• Don't preheat the **CROCK-POT®** slow cooker. Don't place a cold insert into a preheated base.

• Don't place a hot insert on a cold surface or in the refrigerator; don't fill it with cold water.

• Never place stoneware in the freezer.

• Don't use the stoneware insert if it's cracked; replace it.

• For further safety tips, please refer to the instruction manual that came with your **CROCK-POT®** slow cooker.

Starters and Sides

Simple first courses, party appetizers, and traditional side dishes to help round out a meal

Rustic Potatoes au Gratin

MAKES 6 SERVINGS

½ **cup milk**

1 **can (10¾ ounces) condensed Cheddar cheese soup, undiluted**

1 **package (8 ounces) cream cheese, softened**

1 **clove garlic, minced**

¼ **teaspoon ground nutmeg**

⅛ **teaspoon black pepper**

2 **pounds baking potatoes, unpeeled and cut into ¼-inch-thick slices**

1 **small onion, thinly sliced**

Paprika (optional)

1. Heat milk in small saucepan over medium heat until small bubbles form around edge of pan. Remove from heat. Add soup, cream cheese, garlic, nutmeg and pepper. Stir until smooth.

2. Layer one fourth of potatoes and one fourth of onion in **CROCK-POT®** slow cooker. Top with one fourth of soup mixture. Repeat layers 3 times, using remaining potatoes, onion and soup mixture.

3. Cover; cook on LOW 6½ to 7 hours or until potatoes are tender and most of liquid is absorbed. Sprinkle with paprika, if desired.

Ratatouille with Parmesan Cheese

MAKES 4 SERVINGS

Nonstick cooking spray

1 **baby eggplant, diced, *or* 1 cup diced regular eggplant**

2 **medium tomatoes, chopped**

1 **small zucchini, diced**

1 **cup sliced mushrooms**

½ **cup no-salt-added tomato purée**

1 **large shallot *or* ½ small onion, chopped**

1 **clove garlic, minced**

¾ **teaspoon dried oregano**

⅛ **teaspoon dried rosemary**

⅛ **teaspoon black pepper**

2 **tablespoons shredded fresh basil**

2 **teaspoons lemon juice**

¼ **teaspoon salt (optional)**

¼ **cup shredded Parmesan cheese**

1. Coat large skillet with cooking spray. Add eggplant; cook and stir over medium-high heat about 5 minutes until lightly browned.

2. Transfer eggplant to **CROCK-POT®** slow cooker. Add tomatoes, zucchini, mushrooms, tomato purée, shallot, garlic, oregano, rosemary and pepper. Cover; cook on LOW 6 hours.

3. Stir in basil, lemon juice and salt, if desired. Turn off **CROCK-POT®** slow cooker; let stand 5 minutes. Top each serving with 1 tablespoon Parmesan cheese.

Swiss Cheese Scalloped Potatoes

2 **pounds baking potatoes, thinly sliced**

½ **cup finely chopped yellow onion**

¼ **teaspoon salt**

¼ **teaspoon ground nutmeg**

2 **tablespoons butter, cut into small pieces**

½ **cup milk**

2 **tablespoons all-purpose flour**

3 **ounces Swiss cheese slices, torn into small pieces**

¼ **cup finely chopped green onions (optional)**

1. Layer half the potatoes, ¼ cup onion, ⅛ teaspoon salt, ⅛ teaspoon nutmeg and 1 tablespoon butter in **CROCK-POT®** slow cooker. Repeat layers. Cover; cook on LOW 7 hours or on HIGH 4 hours.

2. Remove potatoes with slotted spoon to serving dish and cover with foil to keep warm.

3. Whisk milk and flour in small bowl until smooth. Stir mixture into cooking liquid. Add cheese; stir to combine. Cover; cook on HIGH 10 minutes or until slightly thickened. Stir; pour cheese mixture over potatoes and serve. Sprinkle with green onions, if desired.

Tip: Don't add water to the **CROCK-POT®** slow cooker unless a recipe specifically says so. Foods don't lose much moisture during slow cooking, so follow recipe guidelines.

Mini Carnitas Tacos

MAKES 12 (36 MINI TACOS) SERVINGS

1½ **pounds boneless pork loin, cut into 1-inch cubes**

1 **onion, finely chopped**

½ **cup reduced-sodium chicken broth**

1 **tablespoon chili powder**

2 **teaspoons ground cumin**

1 **teaspoon dried oregano**

½ **teaspoon minced canned chipotle peppers in adobo sauce**

½ **cup pico de gallo**

2 **tablespoons chopped fresh cilantro**

½ **teaspoon salt**

12 **(6-inch) flour or corn tortillas**

¾ **cup (about 3 ounces) shredded sharp Cheddar cheese (optional)**

3 **tablespoons sour cream (optional)**

1. Combine pork, onion, broth, chili powder, cumin, oregano and chipotle peppers in **CROCK-POT®** slow cooker. Cover; cook on LOW 6 hours or on HIGH 3 hours or until pork is very tender. Pour off excess cooking liquid.

2. Shred pork with two forks; stir in pico de gallo, cilantro and salt. Cover and keep warm on LOW or WARM until serving.

3. Cut 3 circles from each tortilla with 2-inch biscuit cutter. Top each with some pork and garnish as desired with Cheddar cheese and sour cream. Serve warm.

Tip: Carnitas, or "little meats" in Spanish, are a festive way to spice up any gathering. Carnitas traditionally include a large amount of lard, but slow cooking makes the dish more healthful by eliminating the need to add lard, oil or fat, while keeping the meat tender and tasteful.

Artichoke and Tomato Paella

MAKES 8 SERVINGS

4 cups vegetable broth

2 cups converted white rice

5 ounces (½ 10-ounce package) frozen chopped spinach, thawed and drained

1 green bell pepper, chopped

1 medium ripe tomato, sliced into wedges

1 medium yellow onion, chopped

1 medium carrot, peeled and diced

3 cloves garlic, minced

1 tablespoon minced fresh parsley

1 teaspoon salt

½ teaspoon black pepper

1 can (13¾ ounces) artichoke hearts, quartered, rinsed and well drained

½ cup frozen peas

1. Combine broth, rice, spinach, bell pepper, tomato, onion, carrot, garlic, parsley, salt and black pepper in **CROCK-POT®** slow cooker. Mix thoroughly. Cover; cook on LOW 4 hours or on HIGH 2 hours.

2. Before serving, add artichoke hearts and peas. Cover; cook on HIGH 15 minutes. Mix well before serving.

Corn on the Cob with Garlic Herb Butter

MAKES 4 TO 5 SERVINGS

½ **cup (1 stick) unsalted butter, softened**

3 **to 4 cloves garlic, minced**

2 **tablespoons finely minced fresh parsley**

4 **to 5 ears of corn, husked**

Salt and black pepper

1. Thoroughly mix butter, garlic and parsley in small bowl.

2. Place each ear of corn on a piece of aluminum foil and generously spread with butter mixture. Season with salt and pepper and tightly seal foil. Place in **CROCK-POT®** slow cooker; overlap ears, if necessary. Add enough water to come one fourth of the way up each ear.

3. Cover; cook on LOW 4 to 5 hours or on HIGH 2 to 2½ hours or until done.

Arizona Black Bean Dip

MAKES 32 SERVINGS

½ **can (about 14 ounces) black beans, drained**

½ **onion, finely diced**

4 **cloves garlic, minced**

1 **tablespoon ground cumin**

1 **teaspoon ground red pepper**

4 **ounces fresh goat cheese, crumbled**

1 **tablespoon green onions, thinly sliced, divided**

2 **tablespoons fresh cilantro, chopped**

Tortilla or corn chips

1. Combine all the ingredients in **CROCK-POT®** **LITTLE DIPPER®** slow cooker, reserving half the green onions. Cover with lid; cook 45 minutes or until cheese is melted, stirring occasionally.

2. Garnish with remaining green onions and serve with tortilla or corn chips.

Tip: For a quicker preparation, place ingredients in a microwave-safe bowl, cover with plastic wrap and poke a fork through the plastic to allow for steam venting. Cook 1½ to 2½ minutes, or until the cheese is melted and bubbly. Spoon dip into **CROCK-POT®** **LITTLE DIPPER®** slow cooker to keep warm for serving.

Herbed Fall Vegetables

MAKES 6 SERVINGS

2 medium Yukon Gold
potatoes, cut into
½-inch dice

2 medium sweet
potatoes, cut into
½-inch dice

3 parsnips, peeled and
cut into ½-inch dice

1 fennel bulb, sliced and
cut into ½-inch dice

½ to ¾ cup chopped fresh
herbs, such as tarragon,
parsley, sage or thyme

¼ cup (½ stick) butter, cut
into small pieces

1 cup chicken broth

1 tablespoon Dijon
mustard

1 tablespoon salt

Black pepper

1. Combine potatoes, parsnips, fennel, herbs and butter in **CROCK-POT®** slow cooker.

2. Whisk together broth, mustard, salt and pepper in small bowl. Pour mixture over vegetables. Cover; cook on LOW 4½ hours or on HIGH 3 hours or until vegetables are tender, stirring occasionally to ensure even cooking.

Spinach, Crab and Artichoke Dip

MAKES 10 SERVINGS

1 can (6½ ounces) crabmeat, drained and shredded

1 package (10 ounces) frozen chopped spinach, thawed and squeezed nearly dry

1 package (8 ounces) reduced-fat cream cheese

1 jar (about 6 ounces) marinated artichoke hearts, drained and finely chopped

¼ teaspoon hot pepper sauce

Melba toast or whole grain crackers (optional)

Pick out and discard any shell or cartilage from crabmeat. Combine crabmeat, spinach, cream cheese, artichokes and hot pepper sauce in 1½-quart **CROCK-POT®** slow cooker. Cover; cook on HIGH 1½ to 2 hours or until heated through, stirring after 1 hour. Serve with melba toast, if desired.

Creamy Red Pepper Polenta

MAKES 4 TO 6 SERVINGS

¼ **cup (½ stick) butter, melted**

¼ **teaspoon paprika, plus additional for garnish**

⅛ **teaspoon ground red pepper**

⅛ **teaspoon ground cumin**

6 **cups boiling water**

2 **cups yellow cornmeal**

1 **small red bell pepper, finely chopped**

2 **teaspoons salt**

Combine butter, paprika, red pepper and cumin in **CROCK-POT**® slow cooker. Add hot water, cornmeal, bell pepper and salt. Stir well to combine. Cover; cook on LOW 3 to 4 hours or on HIGH 1 to 2 hours, stirring occasionally. Garnish with additional paprika, if desired.

Baked Beans

- **2 cans (about 15 ounces each) baked beans**
- **1 cup ketchup**
- **½ cup barbecue sauce**
- **½ cup packed brown sugar**
- **5 slices bacon, chopped**
- **½ green bell pepper, chopped**
- **½ onion, chopped**
- **1½ teaspoons prepared mustard**
- **Fresh parsley (optional)**

Place all ingredients except parsley in **CROCK-POT®** slow cooker. Stir well to combine. Cover; cook on LOW 8 to 12 hours or on HIGH 3 to 4 hours. Garnish with fresh parsley.

Artichoke and Nacho Cheese Dip

MAKES ABOUT 1 QUART

2 cans (10¾ ounces each) condensed nacho cheese soup, undiluted

1 can (14 ounces) quartered artichoke hearts, drained and coarsely chopped

1 cup (4 ounces) shredded or thinly sliced pepper jack cheese

1 can (4 ounces) evaporated milk

2 tablespoons snipped fresh chives, divided

½ teaspoon paprika

Crackers or chips

1. Combine soup, artichoke hearts, cheese, evaporated milk, 1 tablespoon chives and paprika in **CROCK-POT®** slow cooker. Cover; cook on LOW 2 hours.

2. Stir well. Sprinkle with remaining 1 tablespoon chives and serve with crackers.

Orange-Spice Glazed Carrots

MAKES 6 SERVINGS

1 package (32 ounces) baby carrots

½ cup packed light brown sugar

½ cup orange juice

3 tablespoons butter or margarine

¾ teaspoon ground cinnamon

¼ teaspoon ground nutmeg

¼ cup cold water

2 tablespoons cornstarch

1. Combine carrots, brown sugar, orange juice, butter, cinnamon and nutmeg in **CROCK-POT®** slow cooker. Cover; cook on LOW 3½ to 4 hours or until carrots are crisp-tender.

2. Spoon carrots into serving bowl. Transfer cooking liquid to small saucepan. Bring to a boil.

3. Mix water and cornstarch until smooth; stir into saucepan. Boil 1 minute or until thickened, stirring constantly. Spoon over carrots.

Red Hot Applesauce

MAKES 6 SERVINGS

10 to 12 apples, peeled, cored and chopped

¾ cup hot cinnamon candies

½ cup apple juice or water

Combine apples, candies and juice in **CROCK-POT®** slow cooker. Cover; cook on LOW 7 to 8 hours or on HIGH 4 hours or until desired consistency. Serve warm or chilled.

Sweet Potato & Pecan Casserole

MAKES 6 TO 8 SERVINGS

1 can (40 ounces) sweet potatoes, drained and mashed

½ cup apple juice

⅓ cup plus 2 tablespoons butter, melted, divided

½ teaspoon salt

½ teaspoon ground cinnamon

¼ teaspoon black pepper

2 eggs, beaten

⅓ cup chopped pecans

⅓ cup packed brown sugar

2 tablespoons all-purpose flour

1. Combine sweet potatoes, juice, ⅓ cup butter, salt, cinnamon and pepper in large bowl. Beat in eggs. Place mixture into **CROCK-POT®** slow cooker.

2. Combine pecans, brown sugar, flour and remaining 2 tablespoons butter in small bowl. Spread over sweet potatoes in **CROCK-POT®** slow cooker. Cover; cook on HIGH 3 to 4 hours.

Chilies and Chowders

**Hearty and filling winter bowls
to keep you warm**

Three-Bean Turkey Chili

MAKES 6 TO 8 SERVINGS

1 pound lean ground turkey

1 small onion, chopped

1 can (28 ounces) diced tomatoes

1 can (about 15 ounces) chickpeas, rinsed and drained

1 can (about 15 ounces) kidney beans, rinsed and drained

1 can (about 15 ounces) black beans, rinsed and drained

1 can (8 ounces) tomato sauce

1 can (4 ounces) diced mild green chilies

1 to 2 tablespoons chili powder

1. Cook and stir turkey and onion in medium nonstick skillet over medium-high heat until turkey is no longer pink. Drain and discard fat. Transfer to **CROCK-POT**® slow cooker.

2. Add remaining ingredients; mix well. Cover; cook on HIGH 6 to 8 hours.

Red Bliss Potato and Leek Clam Chowder

MAKES 6 TO 8 SERVINGS

4 slices smoked bacon, cut into 1-inch pieces

2 cans (6 ounces each) minced clams, drained and liquid reserved

2 cups Red Bliss* potatoes (peeled and cut into ½-inch cubes)

1 cup finely chopped leeks

1 cup chopped celery

2 carrots, peeled and finely chopped

1 teaspoon sugar

1 teaspoon salt

½ teaspoon black pepper

3 cups cream

2 cups water, divided

1 cup nonfat dry milk

⅓ cup all-purpose flour

1 cup chilled water

Paprika

Red Bliss potatoes are a variety of new red potato grown in California, Minnesota and the Dakotas. If Red Bliss potatoes are unavailable, substitute any new red potato.

1. Heat skillet over medium heat until hot. Add bacon and cook until crisp. Transfer to paper towel-lined plate with slotted spoon to drain excess fat. Cool and reserve in refrigerator for garnish.

2. Place clams in small mixing bowl; cover with plastic wrap and refrigerate.

3. Place reserved clam liquid in **CROCK-POT®** slow cooker. Add potatoes, leeks, celery, carrots, sugar, salt and pepper. Mix well to combine. Stir in cream and 1 cup of water. Cover; cook on LOW 8 hours or on HIGH 4 to 5 hours.

4. Combine dry milk and flour in medium mixing bowl. Gradually whisk in 1 cup chilled water. Add to **CROCK-POT®** slow cooker. Stir well to combine. Cover; cook on HIGH 20 to 30 minutes or until thickened, stirring occasionally. Add reserved clams. Cook 5 minutes longer or until clams are warmed through.

5. Meanwhile, allow reserved bacon to come to room temperature. Serve soup in bowls. Sprinkle with paprika and crumble bacon evenly over each serving.

New England Clam Chowder

MAKES 6 TO 8 SERVINGS

6 **slices bacon, diced**

2 **onions, chopped**

5 **cans (6½ ounces each) clams, drained and liquid reserved**

6 **medium red potatoes, cubed**

2 **tablespoons minced garlic**

1 **teaspoon black pepper**

2 **cans (12 ounces each) evaporated milk**

Salt (optional)

Snipped fresh chives (optional)

1. Cook and stir bacon and onions in medium skillet over medium heat until onions are tender. Place in **CROCK-POT®** slow cooker.

2. Add enough water to reserved clam liquid to make 3 cups. Pour into **CROCK-POT®** slow cooker. Add potatoes, garlic and pepper. Cover; cook on LOW 5 to 8 hours or HIGH 1 to 3 hours.

3. Mix in reserved clams and milk. Cover; cook on LOW 30 to 45 minutes. Add salt to taste, if desired. Garnish with snipped fresh chives, if desired.

Tip: Shellfish and mollusks are delicate and should be added to the **CROCK-POT®** slow cooker during the last 15 to 30 minutes of the cooking time if you're using the HIGH heat setting, and during the last 30 to 45 minutes if you're using the LOW setting. This type of seafood overcooks easily, becoming tough and rubbery, so watch your cooking times, and cook only long enough for foods to be done.

Easy Corn Chowder

MAKES 6 SERVINGS

2 cans (about 14 ounces each) chicken broth

1 bag (16 ounces) frozen corn, thawed

3 small red potatoes, cut into ½-inch pieces

1 red bell pepper, diced

1 medium onion, diced

1 stalk celery, sliced

½ teaspoon salt

½ teaspoon black pepper

¼ teaspoon ground coriander

½ cup heavy cream

8 slices bacon, crisp-cooked and crumbled

1. Place broth, corn, potatoes, bell pepper, onion, celery, salt, black pepper and coriander into **CROCK-POT**® slow cooker. Cover; cook on LOW 7 to 8 hours.

2. Partially mash soup mixture with potato masher to thicken. Stir in cream; cook on HIGH, uncovered, until hot. Adjust seasonings, if desired. To serve, sprinkle on bacon.

Tip: Defrost (frozen) corn before cooking it in the **CROCK-POT**® slow cooker.

Vegetarian Chili

MAKES 4 SERVINGS

- **1 tablespoon vegetable oil**
- **1 cup chopped onion**
- **1 cup chopped red bell pepper**
- **2 tablespoons minced jalapeño peppers***
- **1 clove garlic, minced**
- **1 can (28 ounces) crushed tomatoes, undrained**
- **1 can (about 15 ounces) black beans, rinsed and drained**
- **1 can (about 15 ounces) chickpeas, rinsed and drained**
- **½ cup corn**
- **¼ cup tomato paste**
- **1 teaspoon sugar**
- **1 teaspoon ground cumin**
- **1 teaspoon dried basil**
- **1 teaspoon chili powder**
- **¼ teaspoon black pepper**
- **Sour cream and shredded Cheddar cheese (optional)**

*Jalapeño peppers can sting and irritate the skin, so wear rubber gloves when handling peppers and do not touch your eyes.

1. Heat oil in large skillet over medium-high heat. Add onion, bell pepper, jalapeño peppers and garlic; cook and stir 5 minutes or until tender. Transfer to **CROCK-POT®** slow cooker.

2. Add remaining ingredients except sour cream and cheese; mix well. Cover; cook on LOW 4 to 5 hours.

3. Garnish with sour cream and cheese.

Beggar's Chowder

MAKES 8 SERVINGS

¼ cup (½ stick) unsalted butter, at room temperature

¼ cup all-purpose flour

1 tablespoon garlic salt

1 tablespoon thyme

1 tablespoon sweet Hungarian paprika

½ teaspoon black pepper

4 skinless bone-in turkey legs or thighs, trimmed of visible fat

2 cans (14¾ ounces each) cream-style sweet corn

1 can (10½ ounces) condensed chicken broth, undiluted

1½ cups diced yellow onion

1 cup diced red bell pepper

1 cup diced green bell pepper

1 pound cleaned, stemmed white mushrooms, halved or quartered if large

1 can (about 14 ounces) petite diced tomatoes

1½ cups heavy whipping cream

½ cup chopped fresh cilantro or parsley, plus additional for garnish

Salt and black pepper, to taste

1. Coat **CROCK-POT®** slow cooker with nonstick cooking spray. Combine butter, flour, garlic salt, thyme, paprika and black pepper in small bowl. Use back of wooden spoon to work mixture into smooth paste. Rub paste into all sides of turkey.

2. Place turkey in **CROCK-POT®** slow cooker. Add corn, broth, onion and bell peppers.

3. Cover; cook on HIGH 3 hours or until turkey is fork-tender. Remove turkey; set aside until cool enough to handle.

4. Add mushrooms and tomatoes to cooking liquid. Cover; cook on HIGH 30 minutes.

5. Meanwhile, remove turkey meat from bones in bite-size pieces. When mushrooms are tender, return turkey to **CROCK-POT®** slow cooker. Add cream and cilantro. Cook, covered, about 15 minutes or until heated through. Add salt and pepper, if desired. Garnish with additional chopped cilantro, if desired.

Bean and Corn Chili

MAKES 6 SERVINGS

2 medium onions, finely chopped

5 cloves garlic, minced

½ teaspoon olive oil

2 tablespoons red wine

1 green bell pepper, finely chopped

1 red bell pepper, finely chopped

1 stalk celery, finely sliced

6 plum tomatoes, chopped

2 cans (about 15 ounces each) kidney beans, rinsed and drained

1 can (6 ounces) tomato paste

1 cup frozen corn

1 teaspoon salt

1 teaspoon chili powder

½ teaspoon black pepper

¼ teaspoon ground cumin

¼ teaspoon ground red pepper

¼ teaspoon dried oregano

¼ teaspoon ground coriander

1½ cups fat-free chicken or vegetable broth

1. Cook onions and garlic in oil and red wine in medium skillet until onions are tender. Add onion mixture and remaining ingredients to **CROCK-POT**® slow cooker. Mix thoroughly.

2. Cover; cook on LOW 6 to 8 hours or on HIGH 3 to 4 hours.

Note: Hearty yet low in fat, this chili will warm you on any winter evening.

Tip: Recipe can be doubled for a 5-, 6- or 7-quart **CROCK-POT**® slow cooker.

Chunky Vegetable Chili

MAKES 6 SERVINGS

2 cans (about 15 ounces each) Great Northern beans, rinsed and drained

1 cup frozen corn

1 cup water

1 onion, chopped

2 stalks celery, diced

1 can (6 ounces) tomato paste

1 can (4 ounces) diced mild green chilies, undrained

1 carrot, diced

3 cloves garlic, minced

1 tablespoon chili powder

2 teaspoons dried oregano

½ teaspoon salt

Combine all ingredients in **CROCK-POT®** slow cooker. Cover; cook on LOW 5½ to 6 hours or until vegetables are tender.

Roasted Corn and Red Pepper Chowder

MAKES 4 SERVINGS

2 tablespoons extra-virgin olive oil

2 cups fresh corn or frozen corn, thawed

1 red bell pepper, diced

2 green onions, sliced

4 cups chicken broth

2 baking potatoes, diced

1 teaspoon salt

½ teaspoon black pepper

1 can (13 ounces) evaporated milk

2 tablespoons minced fresh parsley

1. Heat oil in skillet over medium heat until hot. Add corn, bell pepper and onions. Cook and stir until vegetables are tender and lightly browned, about 7 to 8 minutes. Transfer to **CROCK-POT®** slow cooker.

2. Add broth, potatoes, salt and black pepper. Stir well to combine. Cover; cook on LOW 7 to 9 hours or on HIGH 4 to 5 hours.

3. Thirty minutes before serving, add evaporated milk. Stir well to combine and continue cooking. To serve, garnish with parsley.

Chili with Turkey & Beans

MAKES 4 SERVINGS

- **2 cans (about 14 ounces each) whole tomatoes, drained**
- **2 cans (about 15 ounces each) red kidney beans, rinsed and drained**
- **1 pound cooked ground turkey**
- **1 can (about 15 ounces) black beans, rinsed and drained**
- **1 can (12 ounces) tomato sauce**
- **1 cup finely chopped onion**
- **1 cup finely chopped celery**
- **1 cup finely chopped carrot**
- **3 tablespoons chili powder**
- **1 tablespoon Worcestershire sauce**
- **4 teaspoons ground cumin**
- **2 teaspoons ground red pepper**
- **1 teaspoon salt**
- **½ cup amaretto (optional)**
- **Cheddar cheese (optional)**

Combine all ingredients except cheese in **CROCK-POT®** slow cooker. Cover; cook on HIGH 7 hours. Sprinkle with cheese before serving, if desired.

Classic Chili

MAKES 6 SERVINGS

1½ **pounds ground beef**

1½ **cups chopped onion**

1 **cup chopped green bell pepper**

2 **cloves garlic, minced**

3 **cans (about 15 ounces each) dark red kidney beans, rinsed and drained**

2 **cans (about 15 ounces each) tomato sauce**

1 **can (about 14 ounces) diced tomatoes**

2 **to 3 teaspoons chili powder**

1 **to 2 teaspoons ground mustard**

¾ **teaspoon dried basil**

½ **teaspoon black pepper**

1 **to 2 dried red chilies (optional)**

1. Brown ground beef, onion, bell pepper and garlic in large skillet over medium-high heat, stirring to break up meat. Drain fat. Transfer mixture to **CROCK-POT®** slow cooker.

2. Add beans, tomato sauce, tomatoes, chili powder, mustard, basil, black pepper and chilies, if desired; mix well. Cover; cook on LOW 8 to 10 hours or on HIGH 4 to 5 hours.

3. If used, remove chilies before serving.

Mid-Week Dinners

Well-rounded weeknight recipes
to share with your family

Slow Cooker Meat Loaf

MAKES 6 SERVINGS

1½ **pounds ground beef**

¾ **cup milk**

⅔ **cup fine plain dry bread crumbs**

2 **eggs, beaten**

2 **tablespoons minced onion**

1 **teaspoon salt**

½ **teaspoon ground sage**

½ **cup ketchup**

2 **tablespoons packed brown sugar**

1 **teaspoon dry mustard**

1. Combine beef, milk, bread crumbs, eggs, onion, salt and sage in large bowl; shape into ball. Place in **CROCK-POT®** slow cooker. Cover; cook on LOW 5 to 6 hours.

2. Combine ketchup, brown sugar and mustard in small bowl. Pour over meat loaf in **CROCK-POT®** slow cooker. Cover; cook on HIGH 15 minutes.

Herbed Artichoke Chicken

MAKES 6 SERVINGS

1½ **pounds boneless, skinless chicken breasts**

1 **can (about 14 ounces) whole tomatoes, drained and diced**

1 **can (14 ounces) artichoke hearts in water, drained**

1 **small onion, chopped**

½ **cup kalamata olives, pitted and sliced**

1 **cup fat-free chicken broth**

¼ **cup dry white wine**

3 **tablespoons quick-cooking tapioca**

2 **teaspoons curry powder**

1 **tablespoon chopped fresh Italian parsley**

1 **teaspoon dried sweet basil**

1 **teaspoon dried thyme**

½ **teaspoon salt**

½ **teaspoon black pepper**

1. Combine chicken, tomatoes, artichokes, onion, olives, broth, wine, tapioca, curry powder, parsley, basil, thyme, salt and pepper in **CROCK-POT®** slow cooker. Mix thoroughly.

2. Cover; cook on LOW 6 to 8 hours or on HIGH 3½ to 4 hours or until chicken is no longer pink in center.

Note: Inviting flavors of tomato, artichokes, Greek olives and herbs imbue the chicken and tease the appetite!

Tip: For a 5-, 6- or 7-quart **CROCK-POT®** slow cooker, double all ingredients, except for the chicken broth and white wine. Increase the chicken broth and white wine by one half.

Barbecued Beef Sandwiches

MAKES 12 SERVINGS

1 **boneless beef chuck shoulder roast (about 3 pounds)**

2 **cups ketchup**

1 **onion, chopped**

¼ **cup cider vinegar**

¼ **cup dark molasses**

2 **tablespoons Worcestershire sauce**

2 **cloves garlic, minced**

½ **teaspoon salt**

½ **teaspoon ground mustard**

½ **teaspoon black pepper**

¼ **teaspoon garlic powder**

¼ **teaspoon red pepper flakes**

Sesame seed buns, split

1. Cut roast in half; place in **CROCK-POT®** slow cooker. Combine remaining ingredients except buns in large bowl; pour over roast. Cover; cook on LOW 8 to 10 hours or on HIGH 4 to 5 hours.

2. Remove roast from sauce; cool slightly. Trim and discard excess fat from beef. Shred meat using two forks.

3. Let sauce stand 5 minutes to allow fat to rise. Skim off fat.

4. Return shredded meat to **CROCK-POT®** slow cooker. Stir to coat. Cover; cook 15 to 30 minutes or until heated through.

5. Spoon filling into sandwich buns and top with additional sauce, if desired.

Slow Cooker Pepper Steak

MAKES 6 TO 8 SERVINGS

2 tablespoons vegetable oil

3 pounds boneless beef top sirloin steak, cut into strips

1 tablespoon (5 to 6 cloves) minced garlic

1 medium onion, chopped

½ cup reduced-sodium soy sauce

2 teaspoons sugar

1 teaspoon salt

½ teaspoon ground ginger

½ teaspoon black pepper

3 green bell peppers, cut into strips

¼ cup cold water

1 tablespoon cornstarch

Hot cooked white rice

1. Heat oil in large skillet over medium-low heat. Brown steak strips in two batches. Add garlic; cook and stir 2 minutes. Transfer steak strips, garlic and pan juices to **CROCK-POT**® slow cooker.

2. Add onion, soy sauce, sugar, salt, ginger and black pepper to **CROCK-POT**® slow cooker; mix well. Cover; cook on LOW 6 to 8 hours or until meat is tender (up to 10 hours). Add bell pepper strips during final hour of cooking.

3. Blend water and cornstarch until smooth; stir into **CROCK-POT**® slow cooker. Cook, uncovered, on HIGH 15 minutes or until thickened. Serve with rice.

Tip: Cooking times are guidelines. **CROCK-POT**® slow cookers, just like ovens, cook differently depending on a variety of factors. For example, cooking times will be longer at higher altitudes. You may need to slightly adjust cooking times for your **CROCK-POT**® slow cooker.

Spicy Sausage Bolognese Sauce

MAKES 6 SERVINGS

2 tablespoons olive oil, divided

1 pound ground beef

1 pound hot Italian sausage, casings removed

¼ pound pancetta, diced

1 large onion, finely diced

2 medium carrots, peeled and finely diced

1 large stalk celery, finely diced

½ teaspoon salt

½ teaspoon black pepper

3 tablespoons tomato paste

1 tablespoon minced garlic

2 cans (28 ounces each) diced tomatoes

¾ cup whole milk

¾ cup dry red wine

1 pound hot cooked spaghetti (optional)

½ cup grated Parmesan cheese (optional)

1. Heat 1 tablespoon oil in large skillet over medium-high heat. Add ground beef and Italian sausage and cook until no longer pink, stirring often to break up meat. Transfer to **CROCK-POT®** slow cooker with slotted spoon. Discard drippings and wipe out pan with paper towels; return pan to heat.

2. Add remaining 1 tablespoon oil to pan. Add pancetta and cook until crisp and brown, stirring occasionally. Transfer to **CROCK-POT®** slow cooker with slotted spoon.

3. Reduce heat to medium and add onion, carrots, celery, salt and pepper. Cook, stirring occasionally, until onion is translucent and carrots and celery are just tender. Stir in tomato paste and garlic. Cook 1 minute, stirring constantly, then add to **CROCK-POT®** slow cooker. Stir in tomatoes, milk and wine. Cover; cook on LOW 6 hours. Reserve 5 cups sauce for another use. Toss remaining 6 cups sauce with hot cooked spaghetti and sprinkle with Parmesan cheese, if desired, just before serving.

Tarragon Turkey and Pasta

MAKES 4 SERVINGS

1½ to 2 pounds turkey tenderloins

½ cup thinly sliced celery

¼ cup thinly sliced green onions

4 tablespoons fresh tarragon, minced

¼ cup dry white wine

1 teaspoon salt

1 teaspoon black pepper

½ cup plain yogurt

1 tablespoon minced fresh Italian parsley

1 tablespoon lemon juice

2 tablespoons water

1½ tablespoons cornstarch

4 cups pasta of your choice, cooked al dente

1. Combine turkey, celery, green onions, 2 tablespoons fresh tarragon, wine, salt and pepper in **CROCK-POT®** slow cooker. Mix thoroughly. Cover; cook on LOW 6 to 8 hours or on HIGH 3½ to 4 hours or until turkey is no longer pink.

2. Remove turkey; cut into ½-inch-thick medallions. Turn **CROCK-POT®** slow cooker to HIGH. Stir yogurt, remaining 2 tablespoons fresh tarragon, parsley and lemon juice into cooking liquid.

3. Stir water into cornstarch in small bowl. Stir into cooking liquid and cook until thickened. Serve turkey medallions over pasta. Drizzle with tarragon sauce.

Note: This easy dish is elegant enough to serve at a dinner party.

Tip: Recipe can be doubled for a 5-, 6- or 7-quart **CROCK-POT®** slow cooker.

Black Bean Stuffed Peppers

MAKES 6 SERVINGS

Nonstick cooking spray

1 **medium onion, finely chopped**

¼ **teaspoon ground red pepper**

¼ **teaspoon dried oregano**

¼ **teaspoon ground cumin**

¼ **teaspoon chili powder**

1 **can (about 15 ounces) black beans, rinsed and drained**

6 **tall green bell peppers, tops removed**

1 **cup (4 ounces) shredded reduced-fat Monterey Jack cheese**

1 **cup tomato salsa**

½ **cup fat-free sour cream**

1. Spray medium skillet with cooking spray; add onion and cook until golden. Add ground red pepper, oregano, cumin and chili powder.

2. Mash half of black beans with cooked onion in medium bowl. Stir in remaining beans. Place bell peppers in **CROCK-POT**® slow cooker; spoon black bean mixture into bell peppers. Sprinkle cheese over peppers. Pour salsa over cheese. Cover; cook on LOW 6 to 8 hours or on HIGH 3 to 4 hours.

3. Serve each pepper with a dollop of sour cream.

Tip: You may increase any of the recipe ingredients to taste except the tomato soup, and use a 5-, 6- or 7-quart **CROCK-POT**® slow cooker. However, the peppers should fit comfortably in a single layer in your stoneware.

Ratatouille with Chickpeas

MAKES 6 TO 8 SERVINGS

3 tablespoons olive oil, divided

4 cloves garlic, minced

1 yellow onion, cut into ½-inch dice

4 small Italian eggplants, peeled and cut into ¾- to 1-inch dice

Salt and black pepper, to taste

1 red bell pepper, cut into ¾- to 1-inch dice

1 yellow bell pepper, cut into ¾- to 1-inch dice

1 orange bell pepper, cut into ¾- to 1-inch dice

3 small zucchini, cut into ¾-inch dice

1 can (about 15 ounces) chickpeas, rinsed and drained

2 cups crushed tomatoes

¼ cup fresh basil, plus additional for garnish

2 tablespoons chopped fresh thyme

½ to 1 teaspoon red pepper flakes

1. Heat 1 tablespoon oil in skillet on medium-low until hot. Add garlic and onion, and cook 2 to 3 minutes or until translucent. Add eggplants, season with salt and black pepper and cook 1 to 2 minutes. Turn heat to low and cover. Cook 4 to 5 minutes, or until eggplants are tender. Transfer to **CROCK-POT®** slow cooker.

2. Add bell peppers, zucchini and chickpeas.

3. Combine tomatoes, ¼ cup basil, thyme, red pepper flakes and remaining 2 tablespoons oil in medium bowl; stir well. Pour into **CROCK-POT®** slow cooker. Stir together all ingredients. Cover; cook on LOW 7 to 8 hours or on HIGH 4½ to 5 hours or until vegetables are tender. Adjust seasonings. Garnish with additional fresh basil.

Jambalaya

MAKES 6 TO 8 SERVINGS

1 can (28 ounces) whole tomatoes, undrained

1 pound cooked andouille sausage, sliced*

2 cups boiled ham, diced

2 cups water

1 cup uncooked rice

2 onions, chopped

2 stalks celery, sliced

½ green bell pepper, diced

¼ cup tomato paste

2 tablespoons olive or canola oil

1 tablespoon minced garlic

1 tablespoon minced fresh parsley

1 to 2 teaspoons hot pepper sauce, to taste

½ teaspoon dried thyme

2 whole cloves

1 pound medium to large shrimp, peeled, deveined and cleaned

*Or substitute 1 pound cooked smoked sausage or kielbasa.

1. Place all ingredients except shrimp in **CROCK-POT®** slow cooker. Stir well to combine. Cover; cook on LOW 8 to 10 hours or on HIGH 4 to 6 hours.

2. Thirty minutes before serving, turn **CROCK-POT®** slow cooker to HIGH. Add shrimp and continue cooking until shrimp are done. Adjust seasonings, as desired.

Braised Italian Chicken with Tomatoes and Olives

MAKES 4 SERVINGS

2 **pounds boneless, skinless chicken thighs**

1 **teaspoon kosher salt**

½ **teaspoon black pepper**

½ **cup all-purpose flour**

Olive oil

1 **can (about 14 ounces) diced tomatoes**

⅓ **cup dry red wine**

⅓ **cup pitted quartered kalamata olives**

1 **clove garlic, minced**

1 **teaspoon chopped fresh rosemary**

½ **teaspoon red pepper flakes**

Cooked linguini or spaghetti

Grated or shredded Parmesan cheese (optional)

1. Season chicken with salt and black pepper. Spread flour on plate, and lightly dredge chicken in flour, coating both sides.

2. Heat oil in skillet over medium heat until hot. Sear chicken in two or three batches until well browned on both sides. Use additional oil as needed to prevent sticking. Transfer to **CROCK-POT®** slow cooker.

3. Add tomatoes, wine, olives and garlic. Cover; cook on LOW 4 to 5 hours.

4. Add rosemary and red pepper flakes; stir in. Cover; cook on LOW 1 hour. Serve over linguini. Garnish with cheese, if desired.

Chicken Gumbo over Rice

MAKES 6 SERVINGS

4 tablespoons olive oil, divided

½ pound Italian sausage, cut into ¼-inch slices

¼ cup all-purpose flour

1 pound boneless, skinless chicken breasts, cut into ½-inch slices

1 cup chopped onions

1 cup chopped celery

1 cup diced green bell peppers

2 tablespoons minced jalapeño or serrano peppers*

1 teaspoon paprika

1½ cups fresh or frozen okra, cut into ¼-inch slices

1 cup chicken broth

½ cup white wine

2 cups cooked white or brown rice

*Jalapeño and serrano peppers can sting and irritate the skin, so wear rubber gloves when handling peppers and do not touch your eyes.

1. Heat 2 tablespoons oil in skillet over medium heat until hot. Brown and crumble sausage until no pink remains, about 10 minutes. Transfer to paper towel-lined plate with slotted spoon to drain excess fat.

2. Heat remaining 2 tablespoons oil in skillet. Add flour and continuously stir with a whisk. Cook until flour becomes dark brown but not burnt. Add chicken, onions, celery, bell peppers, jalapeño peppers and paprika. Cook and stir 7 to 8 minutes, or until vegetables soften. Transfer to **CROCK-POT**® slow cooker.

3. Add drained sausage, okra, broth and wine. Cover; cook on LOW 7 to 8 hours or on HIGH 4 to 6 hours. Serve over cooked rice.

Classic Pot Roast

MAKES 6 TO 8 SERVINGS

1 tablespoon vegetable
   oil

1 beef chuck shoulder
   roast (3 to 4 pounds)

6 medium potatoes, cut
   into halves

6 carrots, sliced

2 medium onions, cut into
   quarters

2 stalks celery, sliced

1 can (about 14 ounces)
   diced tomatoes

   Salt and black pepper,
   to taste

   Dried oregano

1½ to 2 tablespoons all-
   purpose flour

1. Heat oil in large skillet over medium-low heat until hot. Add roast; brown on all sides. Drain and discard excess fat. Transfer roast to **CROCK-POT®** slow cooker.

2. Add potatoes, carrots, onions, celery and tomatoes. Season with salt, pepper and oregano to taste. Add enough water to cover bottom of **CROCK-POT®** slow cooker by about ½ inch. Cover; cook on LOW 8 to 10 hours.

3. Transfer roast and vegetables to serving platter. To make gravy, whisk together cooking liquid and flour in small saucepan. Cook and stir over medium heat until thickened. Serve over roast and vegetables.

Barbecued Pulled Pork Sandwiches

MAKES 8 SERVINGS

1 pork shoulder roast
(2½ pounds)

1 bottle (14 ounces)
barbecue sauce

1 tablespoon fresh lemon
juice

1 teaspoon packed brown
sugar

1 medium onion, chopped

8 sandwich rolls or
hamburger buns

1. Place pork roast in **CROCK-POT®** slow cooker. Cover; cook on LOW 10 to 12 hours or on HIGH 5 to 6 hours.

2. Remove pork roast from **CROCK-POT®** slow cooker. Shred with two forks. Discard cooking liquid. Return pork to **CROCK-POT®** slow cooker; add barbecue sauce, lemon juice, brown sugar and onion. Cover; cook on LOW 2 hours or on HIGH 1 hour. Serve pork on rolls or buns.

Note: This kid-popular dish is sweet and savory, and most importantly, extremely easy to make. Serve with crunchy coleslaw on the side.

Tip: For a 5-, 6- or 7-quart **CROCK-POT®** slow cooker, double all ingredients except for the barbecue sauce. Increase the barbecue sauce to 1½ bottles (about 21 ounces total).

Shredded Beef Fajitas

MAKES 12 SERVINGS

1 **beef flank steak (about 1½ pounds)**

1 **can (about 14 ounces) diced tomatoes with green chilies**

1 **cup chopped onion**

1 **medium green bell pepper, cut into ½-inch pieces**

2 **cloves garlic, minced** *or* ¼ **teaspoon garlic powder**

1 **package (about 1½ ounces) fajita seasoning mix**

12 **(8-inch) flour tortillas**

Optional toppings: sour cream, guacamole, shredded Cheddar cheese, salsa

1. Cut steak into 6 portions; place in **CROCK-POT**® slow cooker. Combine tomatoes, onion, bell pepper, garlic and fajita seasoning mix in medium bowl. Pour over steak. Cover; cook on LOW 8 to 10 hours or on HIGH 4 to 5 hours or until beef is tender.

2. Remove beef from **CROCK-POT**® slow cooker; shred with two forks. Return beef to **CROCK-POT**® slow cooker and stir.

3. To serve fajitas, place meat mixture evenly into flour tortillas. Add toppings as desired; roll up tortillas.

Like Grandma's Chicken 'n' Dumplings

MAKES 4 TO 6 SERVINGS

2 **cups cooked chicken**

1 **can (10¾ ounces) condensed cream of mushroom soup, undiluted**

1 **can (10¾ ounces) condensed cream of chicken soup, undiluted**

2 **soup cans water**

4 **teaspoons all-purpose flour**

2 **teaspoons chicken bouillon granules**

½ **teaspoon black pepper**

1 **can refrigerated buttermilk biscuits (8 biscuits)**

1. Mix all ingredients except biscuits in **CROCK-POT®** slow cooker.

2. Cut biscuits into quarters and gently stir into mixture. Cover; cook on LOW 4 to 6 hours.

Tip: Don't add water to the **CROCK-POT®** slow cooker, unless the recipe specifically says to do so. Foods don't lose as much moisture during slow cooking as they can during conventional cooking, so follow the recipe guidelines for best results.

Chicken Cacciatore

MAKES 6 TO 8 SERVINGS

¼ cup vegetable oil

2½ to 3 pounds chicken tenders, cut into bite-size pieces

1 can (28 ounces) crushed Italian-style tomatoes, undrained

2 cans (8 ounces each) Italian-style tomato sauce

1 onion, chopped

1 can (4 ounces) sliced mushrooms, drained

2 cloves garlic, minced

1 teaspoon salt

1 teaspoon dried oregano

½ teaspoon dried thyme

½ teaspoon black pepper

Hot cooked spaghetti

1. Heat oil in large skillet over medium-low heat. Working in batches, brown chicken on all sides. Transfer chicken to **CROCK-POT®** slow cooker.

2. Add remaining ingredients except spaghetti. Cover; cook on LOW 6 to 8 hours. Serve over spaghetti.

Broccoli and Beef Pasta

MAKES 4 SERVINGS

2 cups broccoli florets or 1 package (10 ounces) frozen broccoli, thawed

1 onion, thinly sliced

½ teaspoon dried basil

½ teaspoon dried oregano

½ teaspoon dried thyme

1 can (about 14 ounces) Italian-style diced tomatoes

¾ cup beef broth

1 pound lean ground beef

2 cloves garlic, minced

2 cups cooked rotini pasta

¾ cup (about 3 ounces) shredded Cheddar cheese or grated Parmesan cheese, plus additional for garnish (optional)

2 tablespoons tomato paste

1. Layer broccoli, onion, basil, oregano, thyme, tomatoes and broth in **CROCK-POT®** slow cooker. Cover; cook on LOW 2½ hours.

2. Cook and stir beef and garlic in large nonstick skillet over medium-high heat 6 to 8 minutes, stirring to break up meat. Drain fat. Transfer to **CROCK-POT®** slow cooker with tomatoes. Cover; cook on LOW 2 hours.

3. Stir in pasta, cheese and tomato paste. Cover; cook on LOW 30 minutes or until cheese melts and mixture is heated through. Sprinkle with additional cheese, if desired.

Serving Suggestion: Serve with garlic bread.

Scalloped Potatoes and Ham

MAKES 5 TO 6 SERVINGS

6 **large russet potatoes, unpeeled and sliced into ¼-inch rounds**

1 **ham steak (about 1½ pounds), cut into cubes**

1 **can (10¾ ounces) condensed cream of mushroom soup, undiluted**

1 **soup can water**

1 **cup (about 4 ounces) shredded Cheddar cheese**

Grill seasoning, to taste

1. Coat **CROCK-POT®** slow cooker with nonstick cooking spray. Arrange potatoes and ham in layers in **CROCK-POT®** slow cooker.

2. Combine soup, water, cheese and grill seasoning in medium bowl; pour over potatoes and ham. Cover; cook on HIGH about 3½ hours or until potatoes are fork-tender. Turn **CROCK-POT®** slow cooker to LOW and cook 1 hour.

Easy Beef Burgundy

MAKES 4 TO 6 SERVINGS

1½ **pounds boneless beef round steak, cut into 1-inch cubes**

1 **can (10¾ ounces) condensed cream of mushroom soup, undiluted**

1 **cup dry red wine**

1 **onion, chopped**

1 **can (4 ounces) sliced mushrooms, drained**

1 **package (about 1 ounce) dry onion soup mix**

1 **tablespoon minced garlic**

Hot cooked egg noodles

Combine all ingredients in **CROCK-POT®** slow cooker. Cover; cook on LOW 6 to 8 hours or until beef is tender. Serve over noodles.

Carne Rellenos

MAKES 6 SERVINGS

1 can (4 ounces) whole mild green chilies, drained

4 ounces cream cheese, softened

1 flank steak (about 2 pounds)

1½ cups salsa verde

1. Slit whole chilies open on one side with sharp knife; stuff with cream cheese.

2. Open steak flat on sheet of waxed paper; score steak and turn over. Lay stuffed chilies across unscored side of steak. Roll up and tie with kitchen string.

3. Place steak in **CROCK-POT**® slow cooker; pour in salsa. Cover; cook on LOW 6 to 8 hours or on HIGH 3 to 4 hours or until done.

4. Remove steak and cut into 6 pieces. Serve with sauce.

Corned Beef and Cabbage

MAKES 6 TO 8 SERVINGS

12 new red potatoes, quartered

4 carrots, sliced

1 corned beef brisket (about 4 pounds)

2 onions, sliced

3 whole bay leaves

8 whole black peppercorns

1 head cabbage, cut into wedges

1. Place potatoes and carrots in bottom of **CROCK-POT®** slow cooker. Add brisket, onions, bay leaves and peppercorns. Add enough water to cover brisket. Cover; cook on LOW 4 to 5 hours or on HIGH 2 to 2½ hours.

2. Add cabbage. Cover; cook on LOW 4 to 5 hours or on HIGH 2 to 2½ hours. Slice brisket against the grain; serve with vegetables.

Chicken Parisienne

MAKES 6 SERVINGS

6 **boneless, skinless chicken breasts (about 1½ pounds), cubed**

½ **teaspoon salt**

½ **teaspoon black pepper**

½ **teaspoon paprika**

1 **can (10¾ ounces) condensed cream of mushroom or cream of chicken soup, undiluted**

2 **cans (4 ounces each) sliced mushrooms, drained**

½ **cup dry white wine**

1 **container (8 ounces) sour cream**

Hot cooked egg noodles

1. Place chicken in **CROCK-POT**® slow cooker. Sprinkle with salt, pepper and paprika. Add soup, mushrooms and wine; mix well. Cover; cook on HIGH 2 to 3 hours.

2. Add sour cream during last 30 minutes of cooking. Serve over noodles.

Macaroni and Cheese

MAKES 6 TO 8 SERVINGS

6 cups cooked elbow macaroni

2 tablespoons butter

6 cups (24 ounces) shredded Cheddar cheese

4 cups evaporated milk

2 teaspoons salt

½ teaspoon black pepper

Toss macaroni with butter in large bowl. Stir in cheese, evaporated milk, salt and pepper. Transfer to **CROCK-POT®** slow cooker. Cover; cook on HIGH 2 to 3 hours.

Tip: Make this mac 'n' cheese recipe more fun by adding some tasty mix-ins. Diced green or red bell pepper, peas, hot dog slices, chopped tomato, browned ground beef or chopped onion are all great options. Be creative!

Autumn Chicken

MAKES 10 TO 12 SERVINGS

1 **can (14 ounces) whole artichoke hearts, drained**

1 **can (14 ounces) whole mushrooms, divided**

12 **boneless, skinless chicken breasts**

1 **jar (6½ ounces) marinated artichoke hearts, undrained**

¾ **cup white wine**

½ **cup balsamic vinaigrette**

Hot cooked egg noodles

Paprika (optional)

Spread whole artichokes over bottom of **CROCK-POT**® slow cooker. Top with half of mushrooms. Layer chicken over mushrooms. Add marinated artichoke hearts with liquid. Add remaining mushrooms. Pour in wine and vinaigrette. Cover; cook on LOW 4 to 5 hours. Serve over noodles. Garnish with paprika.

Soups and Stews

Effortless soup and stew recipes that are ideal for fall and winter nights

Cauliflower Soup

MAKES 8 SERVINGS

2 heads cauliflower, cut into small florets

8 cups chicken broth

¾ cup chopped celery

¾ cup chopped onion

2 teaspoons salt

2 teaspoons black pepper

2 cups milk or light cream

1 teaspoon Worcestershire sauce

1. Combine cauliflower, broth, celery, onions, salt and pepper in **CROCK-POT®** slow cooker. Cover; cook on LOW 7 to 8 hours or on HIGH 3 to 4 hours.

2. Process soup until smooth using hand mixer or immersion blender. Add milk and Worcestershire sauce; process until blended. Cover; cook on HIGH 15 to 20 minutes or until heated through.

Pasta Fagioli Soup

MAKES 5 TO 6 SERVINGS

2 cans (about 14 ounces each) reduced-sodium beef or vegetable broth

1 can (about 15 ounces) Great Northern beans, rinsed and drained

1 can (about 14 ounces) diced tomatoes

2 zucchini, quartered lengthwise and sliced

1 tablespoon olive oil

1½ teaspoons minced garlic

½ teaspoon dried basil

½ teaspoon dried oregano

½ cup uncooked ditalini, tubetti or small shell pasta

½ cup garlic seasoned croutons

½ cup grated Asiago or Romano cheese

3 tablespoons chopped fresh basil or Italian parsley (optional)

1. Combine broth, beans, tomatoes, zucchini, oil, garlic, dried basil and oregano in **CROCK-POT®** slow cooker; mix well. Cover; cook on LOW 3 to 4 hours.

2. Stir in pasta. Cover; cook on LOW 1 hour or until pasta is tender.

3. Serve soup with croutons and cheese. Garnish with fresh basil.

Tip: Only small pasta varieties like ditalini, tubetti or small shell-shaped pasta should be used in this recipe. The low heat of a **CROCK-POT®** slow cooker won't allow larger pasta shapes to cook completely.

Caramelized French Onion Soup

4 **extra-large sweet onions, peeled**

¼ **cup (½ stick) butter**

2 **cups dry white wine**

8 **cups beef or vegetable broth**

2 **cups water**

1 **tablespoon minced fresh thyme**

6 **slices French bread, toasted**

1 **cup (4 ounces) shredded Swiss or Gruyère cheese**

1. Cut each onion into quarters. Cut each quarter into ¼-inch-thick slices. Heat skillet over medium heat until hot. Add butter and onions. Cook until soft and caramel brown, about 45 to 50 minutes, stirring every 7 to 8 minutes. Transfer to **CROCK-POT®** slow cooker.

2. Add wine to skillet and let liquid reduce to about ½ cup, simmering about 15 minutes. Transfer to **CROCK-POT®** slow cooker.

3. Add broth, water and thyme to **CROCK-POT®** slow cooker. Cover; cook on HIGH 2½ hours or until thoroughly heated.

4. To serve, ladle soup into individual ovenproof soup bowls. Float one slice of toast in each bowl and sprinkle with cheese. Preheat oven broiler and place bowls on top shelf of oven. Broil 3 to 5 minutes, or until cheese is melted and golden. Serve immediately.

Plantation Peanut Soup

MAKES 8 SERVINGS

6 **cups chicken broth**

2 **cups light cream**

1 **cup chunky peanut butter**

1 **cup chopped peanuts, divided**

½ **cup chopped onion**

½ **cup chopped celery**

¼ **cup (½ stick) butter**

½ **teaspoon salt**

½ **cup all-purpose flour**

½ **cup water**

1. Combine broth, cream, peanut butter, ½ cup peanuts, onion, celery, butter and salt in **CROCK-POT®** slow cooker. Cover; cook on LOW 4 hours.

2. Turn **CROCK-POT®** slow cooker to HIGH. Whisk together flour and water, and add to soup. Stir well to combine. Cover; cook on HIGH 20 to 25 minutes or until thickened, stirring occasionally.

3. To serve, garnish with remaining chopped peanuts.

Beef Bourguignon

6 strips bacon, cut into 1- to 2-inch pieces

3 pounds beef rump roast, cut into 1-inch cubes

1 large carrot, peeled and sliced

1 medium onion, sliced

1 teaspoon salt

½ teaspoon black pepper

3 tablespoons all-purpose flour

1 can (10 ounces) condensed beef broth

2 cups red or Burgundy wine

1 pound mushrooms, sliced

½ pound small white onions, peeled

1 tablespoon tomato paste

2 cloves garlic, minced

½ teaspoon dried thyme

1 whole bay leaf

1. Cook bacon in skillet over medium heat until crisp. Remove; set aside.

2. Add beef to skillet and brown well. Remove; set aside.

3. Brown carrot and sliced onion in skillet. Transfer to **CROCK-POT®** slow cooker. Season with salt and pepper. Stir in flour; add broth and mix well. Stir in beef and bacon.

4. Add wine, mushrooms, white onions, tomato paste, garlic, thyme and bay leaf. Cover; cook on LOW 10 to 12 hours or HIGH 5 to 6 hours. Remove and discard bay leaf before serving.

Wild Mushroom Beef Stew

MAKES 5 SERVINGS

1½ to 2 pounds beef stew meat, cut into 1-inch cubes

 2 tablespoons all-purpose flour

 ½ teaspoon salt

 ½ teaspoon black pepper

1½ cups beef broth

 1 teaspoon Worcestershire sauce

 1 clove garlic, minced

 1 bay leaf

 1 teaspoon paprika

 4 shiitake mushrooms, sliced

 2 medium carrots, sliced

 2 medium potatoes, diced

 1 small white onion, chopped

 1 stalk celery, sliced

1. Place beef in **CROCK-POT**® slow cooker. Mix together flour, salt and pepper and sprinkle over meat; stir to coat each piece of meat with flour. Add remaining ingredients and stir to mix well.

2. Cover; cook on LOW 10 to 12 hours or on HIGH 4 to 6 hours. Remove and discard bay leaf. Stir stew before serving.

Note: This classic beef stew is given a twist with the addition of flavorful shiitake mushrooms. If shiitake mushrooms are unavailable in your local grocery store, you can substitute other mushrooms of your choice. For extra punch, add a few dried porcini mushrooms to the stew.

Tip: You may double the amount of meat, mushrooms, carrots, potatoes, onion and celery for a 5-, 6- or 7-quart **CROCK-POT**® slow cooker.

Chicken Tortilla Soup

MAKES 4 TO 6 SERVINGS

4 **boneless, skinless chicken thighs**

2 **cans (about 14 ounces each) diced tomatoes**

1 **can (4 ounces) chopped mild green chilies, drained**

½ **to 1 cup chicken broth**

1 **yellow onion, diced**

2 **cloves garlic, minced**

1 **teaspoon ground cumin**

 Salt and black pepper, to taste

4 **corn tortillas, sliced into ¼-inch strips**

2 **tablespoons chopped fresh cilantro**

½ **cup (2 ounces) shredded Monterey Jack cheese**

1 **avocado, peeled, diced and tossed with lime juice to prevent browning**

 Lime wedges

1. Place chicken in **CROCK-POT**® slow cooker. Combine tomatoes, chilies, ½ cup broth, onion, garlic and cumin in small bowl. Pour mixture over chicken.

2. Cover; cook on LOW 6 hours or on HIGH 3 hours or until chicken is tender. Remove chicken from **CROCK-POT**® slow cooker. Shred with two forks. Return to cooking liquid. Adjust seasonings, adding salt and pepper and more broth, if necessary.

3. Just before serving, add tortillas and cilantro to **CROCK-POT**® slow cooker. Stir to blend. Serve in soup bowls, topping each serving with cheese, avocado and a squeeze of lime juice.

Jerk Pork and Sweet Potato Stew

MAKES 4 SERVINGS

2 tablespoons all-purpose flour

¼ teaspoon salt, or to taste

¼ teaspoon black pepper, or to taste

1¼ pounds pork shoulder, cut into bite-size pieces

2 tablespoons vegetable oil

1 large sweet potato

1 cup frozen or canned corn

¼ cup minced green onions, green parts only, divided

1 clove garlic, minced

½ medium Scotch bonnet chile or jalapeño pepper, cored, seeded and minced (about 1 teaspoon)*

⅛ teaspoon ground allspice

1 cup chicken broth

1 tablespoon lime juice

2 cups cooked rice (optional)

*Scotch bonnet chilies and jalapeño peppers can sting and irritate the skin, so wear rubber gloves when handling and do not touch your eyes.

1. Combine flour, salt and pepper in resealable plastic food storage bag. Add pork and shake well to coat. Heat oil in large skillet over medium heat until hot. Add pork in a single layer (working in two batches, if necessary) and brown on both sides, about 5 minutes. Transfer to **CROCK-POT**® slow cooker.

2. Add sweet potato, corn, 2 tablespoons green onions, garlic, Scotch bonnet pepper and allspice. Stir in broth. Cover; cook on LOW 5 to 6 hours.

3. Stir in lime juice and remaining 2 tablespoons green onions. Adjust salt and pepper to taste. Serve stew over cooked rice, if desired.

Tip: To reduce the amount of fat in **CROCK-POT**® slow cooker meals, trim excess fat from meats and degrease canned broth before using.

Mexican Cheese Soup

MAKES 6 TO 8 SERVINGS

1 pound pasteurized process cheese product, cubed

1 pound ground beef, cooked and drained

1 can (about 15 ounces) kidney beans, undrained

1 can (about 14 ounces) diced tomatoes with green chilies

1 can (about 14 ounces) stewed tomatoes, undrained

1 can (8¾ ounces) corn, undrained

1 envelope taco seasoning

1 jalapeño pepper, seeded and diced* (optional)

Corn chips (optional)

*Jalapeño peppers can sting and irritate the skin, so wear rubber gloves when handling peppers and do not touch your eyes.

1. Coat inside of **CROCK-POT®** slow cooker with nonstick cooking spray. Add cheese, beef, beans, diced tomatoes, stewed tomatoes, corn, taco seasoning and jalapeño pepper, if desired. Mix well.

2. Cover; cook on LOW 4 to 5 hours or on HIGH 3 hours or until done. Serve with corn chips, if desired.

Chicken and Sweet Potato Stew

MAKES 6 SERVINGS

4 boneless, skinless chicken breasts, cut into bite-size pieces

2 medium sweet potatoes, cubed

2 medium Yukon Gold potatoes, cubed

2 medium carrots, peeled and cut into ½-inch slices

1 can (28 ounces) whole stewed tomatoes, undrained

1 teaspoon salt

1 teaspoon paprika

1 teaspoon celery seeds

½ teaspoon black pepper

⅛ teaspoon ground cinnamon

⅛ teaspoon ground nutmeg

1 cup fat-free low-sodium chicken broth

¼ cup fresh basil, chopped

Combine all ingredients except basil in **CROCK-POT®** slow cooker. Cover; cook on LOW 6 to 8 hours or on HIGH 3 to 4 hours. Sprinkle with basil just before serving.

Tip: Recipe can be doubled for a 5-, 6- or 7-quart **CROCK-POT®** slow cooker.

Creamy Sweet Potato and Butternut Squash Soup

MAKES 4 TO 6 SERVINGS

1 pound sweet potatoes, cut into 1-inch cubes (about 3 cups total)

1 pound butternut squash, peeled and diced into 1-inch cubes (about 3½ cups total)

½ cup chopped onion

1 can (about 14 ounces) chicken broth, divided

½ cup (1 stick) butter, cubed

1 can (13½ ounces) coconut milk

½ teaspoon ground cumin

½ teaspoon ground red pepper, or more to taste

1½ teaspoons salt, or more to taste

3 to 4 green onions, finely chopped (optional)

1. Combine sweet potatoes, squash, onion, half of chicken broth and butter in **CROCK-POT®** slow cooker. Cover; cook on HIGH 4 hours or until vegetables are tender.

2. Purée in blender 1 cup at a time until smooth, returning batches to **CROCK-POT®** slow cooker. Stir in remaining broth, coconut milk, cumin, red pepper and salt. To serve, ladle into bowls and sprinkle with chopped green onions, if desired.

Niku Jaga (Japanese Beef Stew)

MAKES 6 TO 8 SERVINGS

2 tablespoons vegetable oil

2 pounds beef stew meat, cut into 1-inch cubes

4 medium carrots, peeled and diagonally sliced

3 medium Yukon Gold potatoes, chopped

1 white onion, peeled and chopped

1 cup water

½ cup Japanese sake or dry white wine

¼ cup sugar

¼ cup soy sauce

1 teaspoon salt

1. Heat oil in skillet over medium heat until hot. Sear beef on all sides, turning as it browns. Transfer beef to **CROCK-POT**® slow cooker.

2. Add remaining ingredients. Stir well to combine. Cover; cook on LOW 10 to 12 hours or on HIGH 4 to 6 hours.

Curried Butternut Squash Soup

MAKES 6 TO 8 SERVINGS

2 pounds butternut squash, rinsed, peeled, cored and chopped into 1-inch cubes

1 firm crisp apple, peeled, seeded and chopped

1 yellow onion, chopped

5 cups chicken broth

1 tablespoon curry powder, sweet or hot

¼ teaspoon ground cloves

Salt and black pepper, to taste

¼ cup chopped dried cranberries (optional)

1. Place squash, apple and onion in **CROCK-POT®** slow cooker.

2. Mix together broth, curry powder and cloves in small bowl. Pour mixture into **CROCK-POT®** slow cooker. Cover; cook on LOW 5 to 5½ hours or on HIGH 4 hours or until vegetables are tender.

3. Process soup in blender, in two or three batches, to desired consistency. Add salt and pepper. Garnish with cranberries, if desired.

Asian Sugar Snap Pea Soup

MAKES 4 SERVINGS

2 tablespoons peanut or canola oil

4 to 5 new potatoes, coarsely chopped

2 green onions, chopped

1 medium carrot, peeled and sliced thin

1 stalk celery, sliced thin

1 leek, sliced thin

5 cups water

2 cups broccoli, washed and cut into florets

1 tablespoon lemon juice

1 tablespoon soy sauce

1 teaspoon ground coriander

1 teaspoon ground cumin

1 teaspoon prepared horseradish

⅛ teaspoon ground red pepper

1 cup fresh sugar snap peas, rinsed and drained

4 cups cooked brown rice

1. Heat oil in skillet over medium heat until hot. Add potatoes, onions, carrot, celery and leek; cook and stir 10 to 12 minutes, or until vegetables begin to soften.

2. Transfer to **CROCK-POT**® slow cooker. Add water, broccoli, lemon juice, soy sauce, coriander, cumin, horseradish and red pepper. Cover; cook on LOW 5 to 6 hours or on HIGH 2 to 3 hours.

3. Add sugar snap peas and stir again. Heat on HIGH until snap peas are tender-crisp, about 15 minutes. To serve, portion rice into 4 bowls. Ladle soup over rice and serve immediately.

French Onion Soup

MAKES 8 SERVINGS

¼ cup (½ stick) butter

3 pounds yellow onions, sliced

1 tablespoon sugar

2 to 3 tablespoons dry white wine or water (optional)

2 quarts (8 cups) beef broth

8 to 16 slices French bread (optional)

½ cup (2 ounces) shredded Gruyère or Swiss cheese

1. Melt butter in large skillet over medium-low heat. Add onions; cover and cook just until onions are tender and transparent, but not browned, about 10 minutes.

2. Remove cover. Sprinkle sugar over onions. Cook and stir 8 to 10 minutes or until onions are caramelized. Add onions and any browned bits to **CROCK-POT®** slow cooker. If desired, add wine to skillet. Bring to a boil, scraping up any browned bits. Add to **CROCK-POT®** slow cooker. Stir in broth. Cover; cook on LOW 8 hours or on HIGH 6 hours.

3. Preheat broiler. To serve, ladle soup into individual soup bowls. If desired, top each with 1 or 2 bread slices and about 1 tablespoon cheese. Place under broiler until cheese is melted and bubbly.

Variation: Substitute 1 cup dry white wine for 1 cup of beef broth.

Black Bean Chipotle Soup

MAKES 4 TO 6 SERVINGS

1 pound dry black beans

2 stalks celery, cut into ¼-inch dice

2 carrots, cut into ¼-inch dice

1 yellow onion, cut into ¼-inch dice

2 chipotle peppers in adobo sauce, chopped

1 cup crushed tomatoes

1 can (4 ounces) chopped mild green chilies, drained

6 cups chicken or vegetable broth

2 teaspoons ground cumin

Salt and black pepper, to taste

Optional toppings: sour cream, chunky-style salsa, chopped fresh cilantro

1. Rinse and sort beans and place in large bowl; cover completely with water. Soak 6 to 8 hours or overnight. (To quick-soak beans, place beans in large saucepan; cover with water. Bring to a boil over high heat. Boil 2 minutes. Remove from heat; let soak, covered, 1 hour.) Drain beans; discard water.

2. Place beans in **CROCK-POT**® slow cooker. Add celery, carrots and onion.

3. Combine chipotle peppers, tomatoes, chilies, broth and cumin in medium bowl. Add to **CROCK-POT**® slow cooker. Cover; cook on LOW 7 to 8 hours or on HIGH 4½ to 5 hours or until beans are tender. Season with salt and pepper.

4. If desired, process mixture in blender, in two or three batches, to desired consistency. Serve with sour cream, salsa and cilantro, if desired.

Tip: For an even heartier soup, add 1 cup diced browned spicy sausage, such as linguica or chourico.

Chicken Fiesta Soup

MAKES 8 SERVINGS

4 boneless, skinless chicken breasts, cooked and shredded

1 can (about 14 ounces) stewed tomatoes, drained

2 cans (4 ounces each) chopped mild green chilies

1 can (28 ounces) enchilada sauce

1 can (about 14 ounces) chicken broth

1 cup finely chopped onion

2 cloves garlic, minced

1 teaspoon ground cumin

1 teaspoon chili powder

1 teaspoon salt

¾ teaspoon black pepper

¼ cup finely chopped fresh cilantro

1 cup frozen corn

1 yellow squash, diced

1 zucchini, diced

8 tostada shells, crumbled

2 cups (8 ounces) shredded Cheddar cheese

1. Combine chicken, tomatoes, chilies, enchilada sauce, broth, onion, garlic, cumin, chili powder, salt, pepper, cilantro, corn, squash and zucchini in **CROCK-POT®** slow cooker. Cover; cook on LOW 8 hours.

2. Ladle soup into bowls; garnish with crumbled tostada shells and cheese.

Beef Stew

MAKES 6 TO 8 SERVINGS

½ **cup all-purpose flour**

1 **teaspoon salt**

1 **teaspoon black pepper**

4 **pounds boneless beef chuck roast, cut into 1-inch cubes**

 Olive oil

2 **cups dry red or white wine**

1 **cup beef broth**

2 **onions, sliced**

1 **cup sliced mushrooms**

1 **cup fresh Italian parsley, minced**

6 **teaspoons minced garlic**

4 **whole bay leaves**

1. Combine flour, salt and pepper in large bowl. Add beef; toss to coat. Heat oil in large skillet over medium heat. Working in batches, brown beef on all sides. Transfer to **CROCK-POT®** slow cooker.

2. Add remaining ingredients; mix well. Cover; cook on LOW 4 to 6 hours or on HIGH 2 to 3 hours. Remove and discard bay leaves before serving.

Leek and Potato Soup

MAKES 4 TO 6 SERVINGS

6 slices bacon, chopped

5 cups shredded frozen hash brown potatoes

3 leeks, white and light green parts only, cut into ¾-inch pieces

1 can (10¾ ounces) condensed cream of potato soup, undiluted

1 can (about 14 ounces) reduced-sodium chicken broth

2 stalks celery, sliced

1 can (5 ounces) evaporated milk

½ cup sour cream

1. Cook bacon in large skillet over medium-high heat, stirring occasionally, until crisp and browned. Remove with slotted spoon and drain on paper towel-lined plate.

2. Set aside 2 tablespoons bacon. Combine remaining bacon, potatoes, leeks, soup, broth, celery and evaporated milk in **CROCK-POT®** slow cooker. Cover; cook on LOW 6 to 7 hours. Stir in sour cream. Sprinkle each serving with reserved bacon.

Moroccan Chicken Stew

MAKES 4 SERVINGS

1 pound boneless, skinless chicken thighs, cut into 2-inch pieces

½ cup chopped celery

½ cup chopped carrots

2 ounces chopped prunes

½ to ¾ cup white wine

⅓ cup white balsamic vinegar

¼ cup packed brown sugar

2 tablespoons olive oil

3 cloves garlic, minced

3 whole bay leaves

½ teaspoon ground cinnamon

½ teaspoon ground coriander

¼ teaspoon dried oregano

Pinch black pepper

Pinch ground ginger

Place all ingredients in **CROCK-POT®** slow cooker. Cover; cook on LOW 3 to 4 hours. Remove and discard bay leaves before serving.

Soups and Stews

Slow Cooker Beef or Veal Stock

3 to 4 tablespoons vegetable oil, divided

3 to 4 pounds beef or veal bones, preferably marrow or knuckle bones

9 cups water, divided

2 large leeks, thoroughly cleaned, cut into 1-inch pieces

3 carrots, cut into 1-inch pieces

3 cups onions, coarsely chopped

2 stalks celery, cut into 1-inch pieces

1 tablespoon tomato paste

2 fresh thyme sprigs

2 large sprigs fresh Italian parsley

1 whole bay leaf

½ tablespoon black peppercorns

1. Preheat oven to 450°F. Coat large roasting pan with 1 to 2 tablespoons oil. Arrange bones in single layer in pan and roast in middle of oven, turning once or twice, until browned, 30 to 45 minutes.

2. Using tongs, transfer bones to **CROCK-POT®** slow cooker. Add 8 cups water. Discard fat from roasting pan, and add ½ cup water to roasting pan, stirring and scraping up brown bits; add to **CROCK-POT®** slow cooker. Cook on LOW 8 to 10 hours or on HIGH 5 to 6 hours.

3. Coat roasting pan with remaining 1 to 2 tablespoons oil and arrange leeks, carrots, onions and celery in single layer. Roast in middle of oven, stirring once or twice, until golden brown, 20 to 30 minutes. Transfer vegetables to **CROCK-POT®** slow cooker and immediately add remaining ½ cup water to hot pan, stirring and scraping up brown bits, then add to **CROCK-POT®** slow cooker. Add tomato paste, thyme, parsley, bay leaf and peppercorns; cook on HIGH 2 hours.

4. Remove bones with tongs and discard. Pour stock in batches through large sieve into stockpot and discard solids. Allow stock to cool to room temperature and place in refrigerator overnight. Before using or freezing, discard any fat that rises to top of chilled stock.

Note: To quickly cool down stock for safe refrigerator storage, pour strained stock into a stockpot and place in a sink or large bowl of ice, stirring often.

Simmering Hot and Sour Soup

MAKES 4 SERVINGS

2 **cans (about 14 ounces each) chicken broth**

1 **cup chopped cooked chicken or pork**

4 **ounces shiitake mushroom caps, thinly sliced**

½ **cup thinly sliced bamboo shoots**

3 **tablespoons rice wine vinegar**

2 **tablespoons soy sauce**

1½ **teaspoons chili paste** *or* **1 teaspoon hot chili oil**

4 **ounces firm tofu, drained and cut into ½-inch pieces**

2 **teaspoons dark sesame oil**

2 **tablespoons cornstarch**

2 **tablespoons cold water**

Chopped fresh cilantro or sliced green onions

1. Combine broth, chicken, mushrooms, bamboo shoots, vinegar, soy sauce and chili paste in **CROCK-POT®** slow cooker. Cover; cook on LOW 3 to 4 hours or on HIGH 2 to 3 hours or until chicken is heated through.

2. Stir in tofu and sesame oil. Whisk cornstarch into water in small bowl; stir into soup. Cover; cook on HIGH 10 minutes or until thickened. Sprinkle with cilantro.

Classic Entertaining

Impress your guests with festive entrées for dinner parties, holidays, and get-togethers

Sweet and Saucy Ribs

MAKES 4 SERVINGS

2 pounds pork baby back ribs

1 teaspoon black pepper

2½ cups barbecue sauce (not mesquite flavored)

1 jar (8 ounces) cherry jam or preserves

1 tablespoon Dijon mustard

¼ teaspoon salt

Additional salt and black pepper (optional)

1. Trim excess fat from ribs. Rub 1 teaspoon pepper over ribs. Cut ribs into 2-rib portions; place in **CROCK-POT®** slow cooker.

2. Combine barbecue sauce, jam, mustard and ¼ teaspoon salt in small bowl; pour over ribs.

3. Cover; cook on LOW 6 to 8 hours or on HIGH 3 to 4 hours or until ribs are tender. Season with additional salt and pepper, if desired.

Asian Ginger Beef over Bok Choy

MAKES 6 TO 8 SERVINGS

2 tablespoons peanut oil

1½ pounds boneless beef chuck roast, cut into 1-inch cubes

3 green onions, cut into ½-inch slices

6 cloves garlic

1 cup chicken broth

½ cup water

¼ cup soy sauce

2 teaspoons ground ginger

1 teaspoon Asian chili paste

9 ounces fresh udon noodles or vermicelli, cooked and drained

3 cups bok choy, trimmed, washed and cut into 1-inch pieces

½ cup chopped fresh cilantro

1. Heat oil in large skillet over medium-high heat until hot. Sear beef on all sides in batches to prevent crowding, turning each piece as it browns. Sear last batch of beef with onions and garlic.

2. Transfer to **CROCK-POT**® slow cooker. Add broth, water, soy sauce, ginger and chili paste. Stir well to combine. Cover; cook on LOW 7 to 8 hours or on HIGH 3 to 4 hours or until beef is very tender.

3. Just before serving, turn **CROCK-POT**® slow cooker to HIGH. Add noodles to **CROCK-POT**® slow cooker and stir well. Add bok choy and stir again. Cook on HIGH until bok choy is tender-crisp, about 15 minutes.

4. Garnish beef with cilantro and serve while hot.

Layered Mexican-Style Casserole

MAKES 6 SERVINGS

2 cans (about 15 ounces each) hominy, drained*

1 can (about 15 ounces) black beans, rinsed and drained

1 can (about 14 ounces) diced tomatoes with garlic, basil and oregano

1 cup thick and chunky salsa

1 can (6 ounces) tomato paste

½ teaspoon ground cumin

3 (9-inch) flour tortillas

2 cups (8 ounces) shredded Monterey Jack cheese

¼ cup sliced black olives

*Hominy is corn that has been treated to remove the germ and hull. It can be found with the canned vegetables or beans in most supermarkets.

1. Prepare foil handles (see Note). Coat **CROCK-POT®** slow cooker with nonstick cooking spray.

2. Combine hominy, beans, tomatoes, salsa, tomato paste and cumin in large bowl.

3. Press 1 tortilla in bottom of **CROCK-POT®** slow cooker. (Edges of tortilla may turn up slightly.) Top with one third of hominy mixture and one third of cheese. Repeat layers. Press remaining tortilla on top. Top with remaining hominy mixture. Set aside remaining cheese. Cover; cook on LOW 6 to 8 hours or on HIGH 2 to 3 hours.

4. Sprinkle with remaining cheese and olives. Cover; let stand 5 minutes. Pull out tortilla stack with foil handles.

Note: To make foil handles, tear off three (18×2-inch) strips of heavy-duty foil or use regular foil folded to double thickness. Crisscross foil strips in spoke design and place in **CROCK-POT®** slow cooker to make lifting of tortilla stack easier.

Curry Chicken with Mango and Red Pepper

MAKES 4 SERVINGS

6 boneless, skinless chicken thighs or breasts

Salt and black pepper, to taste

Olive oil

1 bag (8 ounces) frozen mango chunks, thawed and drained

2 red bell peppers, diced

⅓ cup raisins

1 shallot, thinly sliced

¾ cup chicken broth

1 tablespoon cider vinegar

2 cloves garlic, crushed

4 thin slices fresh ginger

1 teaspoon ground cumin

½ teaspoon curry powder

½ teaspoon whole cloves

¼ teaspoon ground red pepper (optional)

Fresh cilantro (optional)

1. Rinse, dry and season chicken with salt and black pepper.

2. Heat oil in skillet over medium heat until hot. Add chicken and lightly brown, about 3 minutes per side. Transfer to **CROCK-POT®** slow cooker.

3. Add mango, bell peppers, raisins and shallot. Combine remaining ingredients except cilantro in small bowl, and pour over chicken. Cover; cook on LOW 6 to 8 hours or on HIGH 3 to 4 hours.

4. To serve, spoon mangos, raisins and cooking liquid onto chicken. Garnish with cilantro, if desired.

Pork Loin with Sherry and Red Onions

MAKES 8 SERVINGS

3 **large red onions, thinly sliced**

1 **cup pearl onions, blanched and peeled**

2 **tablespoons unsalted butter or margarine**

2½ **pounds boneless pork loin, tied**

½ **teaspoon salt**

½ **teaspoon black pepper**

½ **cup cooking sherry**

2 **tablespoons chopped fresh Italian parsley**

2 **tablespoons water**

1½ **tablespoons cornstarch**

1. Cook red and pearl onions in butter in medium skillet over medium heat until soft.

2. Rub pork loin with salt and pepper and place in **CROCK-POT®** slow cooker. Add cooked onions, sherry and parsley. Cover; cook on LOW 8 to 10 hours or on HIGH 5 to 6 hours.

3. Remove pork loin; cover and let stand 15 minutes before slicing.

4. Stir water into cornstarch in small bowl until smooth and stir into cooking liquid in **CROCK-POT®** slow cooker. Cook on HIGH 15 minutes or until sauce has thickened. Serve sliced pork loin with onions and sherry sauce.

Note: The mild flavor of pork is awakened by this rich, delectable sauce.

Tip: Double all ingredients except for the sherry, water and cornstarch if using a 5-, 6- or 7-quart **CROCK-POT®** slow cooker.

Basil Chicken Merlot with Wild Mushrooms

MAKES 4 TO 6 SERVINGS

3 tablespoons extra-virgin olive oil, divided

1 roasting chicken (about 3 pounds), skinned and cut into individual pieces

1½ cups thickly sliced cremini mushrooms

1 medium yellow onion, diced

2 cloves garlic, minced

1 cup chicken broth

1 can (6 ounces) tomato paste

⅓ cup Merlot or other dry red wine

2 teaspoons sugar

1 teaspoon ground oregano

¼ teaspoon salt

¼ teaspoon black pepper

2 tablespoons minced fresh basil

3 cups cooked ziti pasta, drained

Grated Romano cheese (optional)

1. Heat 1½ to 2 tablespoons oil in skillet over medium heat until hot. Brown half of chicken pieces on each side about 3 to 5 minutes, turning once. Remove with slotted spoon and repeat with remaining chicken. Set chicken aside.

2. Heat remaining oil in skillet and add mushrooms, onion and garlic. Cook and stir 7 to 8 minutes or until onions are soft. Transfer to **CROCK-POT**® slow cooker. Top with reserved chicken.

3. Combine broth, tomato paste, wine, sugar, oregano, salt and pepper in medium bowl. Pour sauce over chicken. Cover; cook on LOW 7 to 9 hours or on HIGH 3 to 4 hours.

4. Stir in fresh basil. Place pasta in large serving bowl or on platter. Ladle chicken and mushrooms over pasta and spoon extra sauce over all. Garnish with Romano cheese, if desired.

Classic Entertaining

Hearty Beef Short Ribs

MAKES 6 TO 8 SERVINGS

2½ pounds flanken-style beef short ribs, bone-in

1 to 2 tablespoons coarse salt

1 to 2 tablespoons black pepper

2 tablespoons olive oil, divided

2 carrots, cut into ¼-inch dice

2 celery stalks, cut into ¼-inch dice

1 large yellow onion, cut into ¼-inch dice

3 cloves garlic, minced

3 whole bay leaves

⅓ cup red wine

⅓ cup crushed tomatoes

⅓ cup balsamic vinegar

1. Season ribs with salt and pepper. Drizzle with 1 tablespoon oil. Heat remaining 1 tablespoon oil in large skillet. Cook ribs until just browned, about 2 to 3 minutes per side. Transfer ribs to **CROCK-POT**® slow cooker. Add carrots, celery, onion, garlic and bay leaves.

2. Combine wine, tomatoes and vinegar in small bowl. Season with salt and pepper, if desired. Pour mixture into **CROCK-POT**® slow cooker. Cover; cook on LOW 8 to 9 hours or on HIGH 5½ to 6 hours, turning once or twice, until meat is tender and falling off the bone.

3. Remove ribs from **CROCK-POT**® slow cooker. Process sauce in blender to desired consistency. To serve, pour sauce over ribs.

Tip: For a change of pace from ordinary short rib recipes, ask your butcher for flanken-style beef short ribs. Flanken-style ribs are cut across the bones into wide, flat portions. They provide all the meaty flavor of the more common English-style short ribs with smaller, more manageable bones.

Boneless Pork Roast with Garlic

MAKES 4 TO 6 SERVINGS

1 **boneless pork rib roast (2 to 2½ pounds), rinsed and patted dry**

Salt and black pepper, to taste

3 **tablespoons olive oil, divided**

4 **cloves garlic, minced**

4 **tablespoons chopped fresh rosemary**

½ **lemon, cut into ⅛- to ¼-inch slices**

¼ **cup white wine**

½ **cup chicken broth**

1. Unroll pork roast and season with salt and pepper. Combine 2 tablespoons oil, garlic and rosemary in small bowl. Rub over pork.

2. Roll and tie pork snugly with twine. Tuck lemon slices under twine and into ends of roast.

3. Heat remaining 1 tablespoon oil in skillet over medium heat until hot. Sear pork on all sides until just browned. Transfer to **CROCK-POT®** slow cooker.

4. Return skillet to heat. Add wine and broth, stirring with wooden spoon to loosen any caramelized bits. Pour over pork. Cover; cook on LOW 8 to 9 hours or on HIGH 3½ to 4 hours.

5. Transfer roast to cutting board. Allow to rest 10 minutes before removing twine and slicing. Adjust seasonings, if desired. To serve, pour pan juices over sliced pork.

French Beef Bourguignon

- **2 tablespoons vegetable oil**
- **2 pounds boneless beef chuck roast, cut into 1-inch cubes**
- **4 carrots, quartered lengthwise and cut into 4-inch pieces**
- **1 can (about 14 ounces) diced tomatoes**
- **1 yellow onion, diced**
- **2 stalks celery, sliced**
- **1 cup chopped mushrooms**
- **1 cup dry red wine**
- **1 tablespoon chopped fresh thyme**
- **1 teaspoon salt**
- **1 teaspoon minced fresh basil**
- **1 teaspoon ground mustard**
- **¼ teaspoon black pepper**
- **¼ cup water**
- **2 tablespoons all-purpose flour**
- **1 package (16 ounces) wide egg noodles, cooked according to package directions (optional)**

1. Heat oil in large skillet over medium-high heat. Working in batches, brown beef on all sides. Transfer to **CROCK-POT®** slow cooker.

2. Add carrots, tomatoes, onion, celery, mushrooms, wine, thyme, salt, basil, ground mustard and pepper; mix well. Cover; cook on LOW 8 to 10 hours or on HIGH 4 to 5 hours or until beef is tender.

3. Thirty minutes before serving, whisk water into flour in small bowl until smooth. Stir into sauce. Cook, uncovered, on HIGH 5 minutes or until thickened. Serve over noodles, if desired.

Classic Entertaining

Spanish Paella with Chicken and Sausage

1 **tablespoon olive oil**

4 **chicken thighs (about 2 pounds total)**

1 **medium onion, chopped**

1 **clove garlic, minced**

1 **pound hot smoked sausage, sliced into rounds**

1 **can (about 14 ounces) stewed tomatoes, undrained**

1 **cup arborio rice**

4 **cups chicken broth**

Pinch saffron (optional)

½ **cup frozen peas, thawed**

1. Heat oil in large skillet over medium-high heat until hot. Add chicken in batches and brown well on all sides. Transfer chicken to **CROCK-POT®** slow cooker as it browns.

2. Add onion to same skillet and cook until translucent. Stir in garlic, sausage, tomatoes, rice and broth. Stir in saffron, if desired. Pour over chicken. Cover; cook on LOW 6 to 8 hours or on HIGH 3 to 4 hours or until chicken is fully cooked and rice is tender.

3. Remove chicken to serving platter and fluff rice with fork. Stir in peas. Spoon rice onto platter with chicken.

Golden Pork with Cinnamon-Sugar Apples

MAKES 6 SERVINGS

1 pork sirloin roast
(about 3 pounds)

1 can (10¾ ounces)
condensed golden
mushroom soup,
undiluted

½ cup water

¼ cup packed brown sugar

2 tablespoons soy sauce

¼ cup granulated sugar

3 tablespoons ground
cinnamon

2 Granny Smith apples,
cored and sliced

Hot cooked noodles or
rice

1. Place pork in **CROCK-POT**® slow cooker.

2. Combine soup, water, brown sugar and soy sauce in medium bowl; stir to mix well. Pour over pork. Cover; cook on LOW 8 hours.

3. About 1 hour before serving, combine granulated sugar and cinnamon in medium resealable plastic food storage bag. Add apples; shake to coat well. Place apples on top of pork. Cover; cook 1 hour. Serve with noodles or rice.

Italian-Style Pot Roast

MAKES 6 TO 8 SERVINGS

2 **teaspoons minced garlic**

1 **teaspoon salt**

1 **teaspoon dried basil**

1 **teaspoon dried oregano**

¼ **teaspoon red pepper flakes**

1 **boneless beef bottom round rump or chuck shoulder roast (about 2½ to 3 pounds)**

1 **large onion, quartered and thinly sliced**

1½ **cups tomato-basil or marinara pasta sauce**

2 **cans (about 15 ounces each) cannellini or Great Northern beans, rinsed and drained**

¼ **cup shredded fresh basil**

1. Combine garlic, salt, dried basil, oregano and red pepper flakes in small bowl; rub over roast.

2. Place half of onion slices into **CROCK-POT®** slow cooker. (Cut roast in half to fit into smaller **CROCK-POT®** slow cooker.) Place half of roast over onion slices; top with remaining onion slices and other half of roast (if using 4-quart **CROCK-POT®** slow cooker). Pour pasta sauce over roast. Cover; cook on LOW 8 to 9 hours or until roast is fork-tender.

3. Remove roast to cutting board; tent with foil. Let liquid in **CROCK-POT®** slow cooker stand 5 minutes to allow fat to rise. Skim off fat.

4. Stir beans into liquid. Cover; cook on LOW 15 to 30 minutes or until beans are hot. Carve roast across the grain into thin slices. Serve with bean mixture and fresh basil.

Coq au Vin

MAKES 6 SERVINGS

- 2 **cups frozen pearl onions, thawed**
- 4 **slices thick-cut bacon, crisp-cooked and crumbled**
- 1 **cup sliced mushrooms**
- 1 **clove garlic, minced**
- 1 **teaspoon dried thyme**
- ⅛ **teaspoon black pepper**
- 6 **boneless, skinless chicken breasts (about 2 pounds)**
- ½ **cup dry red wine**
- ¾ **cup reduced-sodium chicken broth**
- ¼ **cup tomato paste**
- 3 **tablespoons all-purpose flour**

  Hot cooked egg noodles (optional)

1. Layer onions, bacon, mushrooms, garlic, thyme, pepper, chicken, wine and broth in **CROCK-POT®** slow cooker. Cover; cook on LOW 6 to 8 hours.

2. Remove chicken and vegetables; cover and keep warm. Ladle ½ cup cooking liquid into small bowl; cool slightly. Mix reserved liquid, tomato paste and flour until smooth; stir into **CROCK-POT®** slow cooker. Turn **CROCK-POT®** slow cooker to HIGH. Cook, uncovered, 15 minutes or until thickened. Serve over hot noodles, if desired.

Note: Coq au Vin is a classic French dish that is traditionally made with bone-in chicken, salt pork or bacon, brandy, red wine and herbs. The dish originated when farmers needed a way to cook old chickens that could no longer breed. A slow, moist cooking method was needed to tenderize the tough old birds.

Barbecue Ribs

MAKES 6 SERVINGS

Canola oil or vegetable oil

2 small red onions, finely chopped

3 to 4 cloves garlic, minced

1 cup ketchup

1 cup packed brown sugar

½ cup cider vinegar

Juice of 1 lemon

2 tablespoons Worcestershire sauce

1 tablespoon hot pepper sauce, or to taste

½ teaspoon chili powder

2 racks pork baby back ribs, cut into 3- to 4-rib sections

1. Heat oil in skillet over medium heat until hot. Add onions and garlic. Cook and stir until softened and lightly browned. Stir in ketchup, brown sugar, vinegar, lemon juice, Worcestershire sauce, hot pepper sauce and chili powder. Simmer gently about w5 minutes. Remove half of sauce and reserve.

2. Transfer remaining sauce to **CROCK-POT**® slow cooker. Add ribs, stirring to coat. Cover; cook on LOW 7 to 9 hours or on HIGH 4 to 6 hours. To serve, cut ribs between bones and pass reserved sauce.

Boneless Chicken Cacciatore

MAKES 6 SERVINGS

Olive oil

6 boneless, skinless chicken breasts, sliced in half horizontally

4 cups tomato-basil sauce or marinara sauce

1 cup coarsely chopped yellow onion

1 cup coarsely chopped green bell pepper

1 can (6 ounces) sliced mushrooms

¼ cup dry red wine (optional)

2 teaspoons minced garlic

2 teaspoons dried oregano, crushed

2 teaspoons dried thyme, crushed

2 teaspoons salt

2 teaspoons black pepper

1. Heat oil in skillet over medium heat until hot. Brown chicken on both sides, turning as it browns. Drain and transfer to **CROCK-POT®** slow cooker.

2. Add remaining ingredients, and stir well to combine. Cover; cook on LOW 5 to 7 hours or on HIGH 2 to 3 hours.

Chicken Provençal

MAKES 8 SERVINGS

2 **pounds boneless, skinless chicken thighs, each cut into quarters**

2 **medium red bell peppers, cut into ¼-inch-thick slices**

1 **medium yellow bell pepper, cut into ¼-inch-thick slices**

1 **onion, thinly sliced**

1 **can (28 ounces) plum tomatoes, drained**

3 **cloves garlic, minced**

¼ **teaspoon salt**

¼ **teaspoon thyme**

¼ **teaspoon fennel seeds, crushed**

3 **strips orange peel**

½ **cup fresh basil, shredded**

Place chicken, bell peppers, onion, tomatoes, garlic, salt, thyme, fennel seeds and orange peel in **CROCK-POT®** slow cooker. Mix thoroughly. Cover; cook on LOW 7 to 9 hours or on HIGH 3 to 4 hours. Sprinkle with basil to serve.

Note: This Southern French chicken dish contrasts the citrus with the sweet. Serve with a crusty French baguette and seasonal vegetables.

Tip: Recipe can be doubled for a 5-, 6- or 7-quart **CROCK-POT®** slow cooker.

Cajun Chicken and Shrimp Creole

MAKES 6 SERVINGS

1 pound skinless chicken thighs

1 red bell pepper, chopped

1 large onion, chopped

1 stalk celery, diced

1 can (about 15 ounces) stewed tomatoes, undrained and chopped

1 clove garlic, minced

1 tablespoon sugar

1 teaspoon paprika

1 teaspoon Cajun seasoning

1 teaspoon salt

1 teaspoon black pepper

1 pound raw shrimp, peeled, deveined and cleaned

1 tablespoon fresh lemon juice

Louisiana-style hot sauce, to taste

1 cup prepared quick-cooking rice

1. Place chicken in **CROCK-POT**® slow cooker. Add bell pepper, onion, celery, tomatoes, garlic, sugar, paprika, Cajun seasoning, salt and black pepper. Cover; cook on LOW 8 to 10 hours or on HIGH 4 to 5 hours.

2. In the last hour of cooking, add shrimp, lemon juice and hot sauce. Serve over hot rice.

Note: Enjoy the full flavors of chicken, shrimp and spices in this delicious creole!

Tip: Recipe can be doubled for a 5-, 6- or 7-quart **CROCK-POT**® slow cooker.

Fresh Herbed Turkey Breast

MAKES 8 SERVINGS

2 tablespoons butter, softened

¼ cup fresh sage leaves, minced

¼ cup fresh tarragon, minced

1 clove garlic, minced

1 teaspoon black pepper

½ teaspoon salt

1 (4-pound) split turkey breast

1 tablespoon plus 1½ teaspoons cornstarch

1. Combine butter, sage, tarragon, garlic, pepper and salt in small bowl. Rub butter mixture all over turkey breast.

2. Place turkey breast in **CROCK-POT**® slow cooker. Cover; cook on LOW 8 to 10 hours or on HIGH 4 to 5 hours or until turkey is no longer pink in the center.

3. Transfer turkey breast to serving platter; cover with foil to keep warm. Slowly whisk cornstarch into cooking juices; cook, uncovered, on HIGH until thickened and smooth. Slice turkey breast. Serve sauce on the side.

Note: Fresh herbs enliven this simple, excellent main dish.

Tip: Recipe can be doubled for a 5-, 6- or 7-quart **CROCK-POT**® slow cooker.

Slow-Cooked Beef Brisket Dinner

MAKES 8 TO 10 SERVINGS

1 beef brisket (4 pounds), cut in half

4 to 6 medium potatoes, unpeeled and cut into large chunks

6 carrots, cut into 1-inch pieces

8 ounces mushrooms, sliced

½ large onion, sliced

1 stalk celery, cut into 1-inch pieces

3 cubes beef bouillon

5 cloves garlic, crushed

1 teaspoon black peppercorns

2 whole bay leaves

Water, as needed

Salt and black pepper, to taste

Chopped fresh parsley (optional)

1. Place brisket, potatoes, carrots, mushrooms, onion, celery, bouillon cubes, garlic, peppercorns and bay leaves in **CROCK-POT®** slow cooker. Add enough water to cover ingredients. Cover; cook on LOW 6 to 8 hours.

2. Remove and discard bay leaves. Transfer brisket to cutting board. Season with salt and pepper to taste. Slice meat across grain. Serve with vegetables. Garnish with parsley, if desired.

Pork Tenderloin with Cabbage

MAKES 6 SERVINGS

- **3 cups shredded red cabbage**
- **¼ cup chopped onion**
- **1 clove garlic, minced**
- **1½ pounds pork tenderloin**
- **¾ cup apple juice concentrate**
- **¼ cup chicken broth or water**
- **3 tablespoons honey mustard**
- **1½ tablespoons Worcestershire sauce**

1. Add cabbage, onion and garlic to **CROCK-POT®** slow cooker. Place pork over cabbage mixture. Combine apple juice concentrate, broth, mustard and Worcestershire sauce in small bowl. Pour over pork. Cover; cook on LOW 6 to 8 hours or on HIGH 3 to 4 hours.

2. Slice pork and serve with cabbage and juices.

Shrimp Jambalaya

MAKES 6 SERVINGS

1 can (28 ounces) diced tomatoes

1 medium onion, chopped

1 medium red bell pepper, chopped

1 stalk celery, chopped

2 tablespoons minced garlic

2 teaspoons dried parsley flakes

2 teaspoons dried oregano

1 teaspoon hot pepper sauce

½ teaspoon dried thyme

2 pounds cooked large shrimp

2 cups uncooked instant rice

2 cups fat-free reduced-sodium chicken broth

1. Combine tomatoes, onion, bell pepper, celery, garlic, parsley, oregano, hot pepper sauce and thyme in **CROCK-POT**® slow cooker. Cover; cook on LOW 8 hours or on HIGH 4 hours.

2. Stir in shrimp. Cover; cook on LOW 20 minutes.

3. Meanwhile, prepare rice according to package directions, substituting broth for water. Serve jambalaya over rice.

Roast Ham with Tangy Mustard Glaze

MAKES 12 TO 15 SERVINGS

1 **fully cooked boneless ham (about 3 pounds), trimmed**

¼ **cup packed dark brown sugar**

2 **tablespoons lemon juice, divided**

1 **tablespoon Dijon mustard**

½ **teaspoon ground allspice**

¼ **cup granulated sugar**

2 **tablespoons cornstarch**

1. Place ham in **CROCK-POT®** slow cooker. Combine brown sugar, 2 teaspoons lemon juice, mustard and allspice. Spoon evenly over ham. Cover; cook on LOW 6 to 7 hours or until ham is heated through and sauce is absorbed. Transfer ham to warm serving platter.

2. Pour cooking liquid from **CROCK-POT®** slow cooker into small heavy saucepan. Add granulated sugar, cornstarch and remaining lemon juice. Bring to a boil over medium-high heat. Reduce heat to medium; cook and stir until sauce is thickened and glossy.

3. Carve ham into slices. Serve with sauce.

Shrimp Creole

MAKES 8 TO 10 SERVINGS

¼ cup (½ stick) butter

1 onion, chopped

¼ cup biscuit baking mix

3 cups water

2 cans (6 ounces each) tomato paste

1 cup chopped celery

1 cup chopped green bell pepper

2 teaspoons salt

½ teaspoon sugar

2 whole bay leaves

Black pepper, to taste

4 pounds raw shrimp, peeled, deveined and cleaned

Hot cooked rice

1. Cook and stir butter and onion in medium skillet over medium heat until onion is tender. Stir in biscuit mix. Place mixture in **CROCK-POT®** slow cooker.

2. Add water, tomato paste, celery, bell pepper, salt, sugar, bay leaves and black pepper. Cover; cook on LOW 6 to 8 hours.

3. Turn **CROCK-POT®** slow cooker to HIGH and add shrimp. Cook on HIGH 45 minutes to 1 hour or until shrimp are done. Remove and discard bay leaves. Serve over rice.

Cashew Chicken

MAKES 6 SERVINGS

- **6 boneless, skinless chicken breasts**
- **1½ cups cashew nuts**
- **1 cup sliced mushrooms**
- **1 cup sliced celery**
- **1 can (10¾ ounces) condensed cream of mushroom soup, undiluted**
- **¼ cup chopped green onions**
- **2 tablespoons butter**
- **1½ tablespoons soy sauce**
- **Hot cooked rice**

Combine chicken, cashews, mushrooms, celery, soup, onions, butter and soy sauce in **CROCK-POT®** slow cooker. Cover; cook on LOW 6 to 8 hours or on HIGH 4 to 6 hours or until done. Serve over rice.

Sweet Endings

Brownie Bottoms

MAKES 6 SERVINGS

¾ **cup water**

½ **cup packed brown sugar**

2 **tablespoons unsweetened cocoa powder**

2½ **cups packaged brownie mix**

1 **package (2¾ ounces) instant chocolate pudding mix**

½ **cup milk chocolate chips**

2 **eggs, beaten**

3 **tablespoons butter or margarine, melted**

1. Lightly coat **CROCK-POT**® slow cooker with nonstick cooking spray. Combine water, brown sugar and cocoa powder in small saucepan over medium heat; bring to a boil over medium-high heat.

2. Meanwhile, combine brownie mix, pudding mix, chocolate chips, eggs and butter in medium bowl; stir until well blended. Spread batter in bottom of **CROCK-POT**® slow cooker; pour boiling sugar mixture over batter. Cover; cook on HIGH 1½ hours.

3. Turn off **CROCK-POT**® slow cooker and let stand for 30 minutes before serving. Serve warm.

Note: Serve this warm chocolate dessert with whipped cream or ice cream.

Tip: Recipe can be doubled for a 5-, 6- or 7-quart **CROCK-POT**® slow cooker.

Banana Nut Bread

MAKES 6 SERVINGS

⅓ **cup butter or margarine**

⅔ **cup sugar**

2 **eggs, well beaten**

2 **tablespoons dark corn syrup**

3 **ripe bananas, well mashed**

1¾ **cups all-purpose flour**

2 **teaspoons baking powder**

½ **teaspoon salt**

¼ **teaspoon baking soda**

½ **cup chopped walnuts**

1. Grease and flour inside of **CROCK-POT**® slow cooker. Beat butter in large bowl with electric mixer until light and fluffy. Slowly add sugar, eggs, corn syrup and mashed bananas. Beat until smooth.

2. Sift together flour, baking powder, salt and baking soda in small bowl. Slowly beat flour mixture into banana mixture. Add walnuts and mix thoroughly. Pour into **CROCK-POT**® slow cooker. Cover; cook on HIGH 2 to 3 hours.

3. Let cool, then turn bread out onto serving platter.

Note: Banana nut bread has always been a favorite way to use up those overripe bananas. Not only is it delicious, but it also freezes well for future use.

Tip: Recipe can be doubled for a 5-, 6- or 7-quart **CROCK-POT**® slow cooker.

Sweet Endings

English Bread Pudding

MAKES 6 TO 8 SERVINGS

16 slices day-old, firm-textured white bread (1 small loaf)

1¾ cups milk

1 package (8 ounces) mixed dried fruit, cut into small pieces

½ cup chopped nuts

1 medium apple, cored and chopped

⅓ cup packed brown sugar

¼ cup (½ stick) butter, melted

1 egg, lightly beaten

1 teaspoon ground cinnamon

¼ teaspoon ground nutmeg

¼ teaspoon ground cloves

1. Tear bread, with crusts, into 1- to 2-inch pieces; place in **CROCK-POT®** slow cooker. Pour milk over bread; let soak 30 minutes. Stir in dried fruit, nuts and apple.

2. Combine remaining ingredients in small bowl; pour over bread mixture. Stir well to blend. Cover; cook on LOW 3½ to 4 hours or until skewer inserted into center of pudding comes out clean.

Note: Chopping dried fruits can be difficult. To make the job easier, cut fruit with kitchen scissors. Spray scissors (or your chef's knife) with nonstick cooking spray before chopping, to prevent sticking.

Blueberry Cobbler

¾ **cup biscuit mix**

½ **cup packed brown sugar**

⅓ **cup granulated sugar**

2 **large eggs**

1 **teaspoon vanilla**

½ **teaspoon almond extract**

1 **can (5 ounces) evaporated milk**

2 **teaspoons melted butter**

3 **cups fresh or frozen blueberries**

Vanilla ice cream, for serving (optional)

1. Coat inside of **CROCK-POT®** slow cooker with nonstick cooking spray. In large bowl, combine biscuit mix and sugars. Add eggs, vanilla and almond extract. Stir to combine. Add evaporated milk and butter. Stir until fully combined.

2. Pour about one fourth of batter into **CROCK-POT®** slow cooker. Place blueberries on top. Pour remaining batter over blueberries. Cover; cook on LOW 5 to 6 hours. Serve warm with ice cream, if desired.

Five-Spice Apple Crisp

MAKES 4 SERVINGS

3 tablespoons unsalted butter, melted

6 Golden Delicious apples, peeled, cored and cut into ½-inch-thick slices

2 teaspoons fresh lemon juice

¼ cup packed light brown sugar

¾ teaspoon Chinese five-spice powder or ½ teaspoon ground cinnamon and ¼ teaspoon ground allspice

1 cup coarsely crushed Chinese-style almond cookies or almond biscotti

Sweetened whipped cream (optional)

1. Grease 4½-quart **CROCK-POT®** slow cooker with melted butter. Add apples and lemon juice and toss to combine. Sprinkle with brown sugar and five-spice powder and toss again. Cover; cook on LOW 3½ hours or until apples are tender.

2. Sprinkle cookies over apples. Spoon into bowls and serve warm, garnished with whipped cream, if desired.

Cherry Delight

1 can (21 ounces) cherry pie filling

1 package (about 18 ounces) yellow cake mix

½ cup (1 stick) butter, melted

⅓ cup chopped walnuts

Whipped topping or vanilla ice cream (optional)

1. Place pie filling in **CROCK-POT®** slow cooker. Mix together cake mix and butter in medium bowl. Spread evenly over pie filling. Sprinkle walnuts on top. Cover; cook on LOW 3 to 4 hours or on HIGH 1½ to 2 hours.

2. Spoon into serving dishes. Serve warm with whipped topping or ice cream, if desired.

Chocolate Orange Fondue

MAKES 1½ CUPS

½ **cup whipping cream**

1½ **tablespoons butter**

6 **ounces 60 to 70% bittersweet chocolate, coarsely chopped**

⅓ **cup orange liqueur**

¾ **teaspoon vanilla**

Marshmallows, strawberries and pound cake cubes

1. Bring cream and butter to a boil in medium saucepan over medium heat. Remove from heat and stir in chocolate, liqueur and vanilla until chocolate is melted. Place over medium-low heat and cook 2 minutes until smooth, stirring constantly.

2. Coat **CROCK-POT® LITTLE DIPPER®** slow cooker with nonstick cooking spray. Fill with warm fondue. Serve with marshmallows, strawberries and pound cake cubes.

Sweet Endings

Spicy Apple Butter

MAKES ABOUT 6 CUPS

5 pounds tart cooking apples (McIntosh, Granny Smith, Rome Beauty or York Imperial), peeled, cored and quartered (about 10 large apples)

1 cup sugar

½ cup apple juice

2 teaspoons ground cinnamon

½ teaspoon ground cloves

½ teaspoon ground allspice

1. Combine all ingredients in **CROCK-POT®** slow cooker. Cover; cook on LOW 8 to 10 hours or until apples are very tender.

2. Mash apples with potato masher. Cook, uncovered, on LOW 2 hours or until thickened, stirring occasionally to prevent sticking.

Serving Suggestion: Homemade apple butter is a great alternative to store-bought jam or jelly on your favorite toast or muffin. For an instant dessert, try toasting a few slices of pound cake and spreading apple butter on them!

Chai Tea

MAKES 8 TO 10 SERVINGS

2 **quarts (8 cups) water**

8 **bags black tea**

¾ **cup sugar***

16 **whole cloves**

16 **whole cardamom seeds, pods removed (optional)**

5 **cinnamon sticks**

8 **slices fresh ginger**

1 **cup milk**

*Chai tea is typically sweet. For less-sweet tea, reduce sugar to ½ cup.

1. Combine water, tea, sugar, cloves, cardamom, if desired, cinnamon and ginger in **CROCK-POT®** slow cooker. Cover; cook on HIGH 2 to 2½ hours.

2. Strain mixture; discard solids. (At this point, tea may be covered and refrigerated up to 3 days.)

3. Stir in milk just before serving. Serve warm or chilled.

Recipe Index

Carne Rellenos (page 83)

Recipe Index

**Chunky
Vegetable Chili
(page 42)**

French Onion Soup (page 116)

Recipe Index

**Shrimp Creole
(page 168)**

Recipe Index

Metric Chart

VOLUME MEASUREMENTS (dry)

$^1\!/_8$ teaspoon = 0.5 mL
$^1\!/_4$ teaspoon = 1 mL
$^1\!/_2$ teaspoon = 2 mL
$^3\!/_4$ teaspoon = 4 mL
1 teaspoon = 5 mL
1 tablespoon = 15 mL
2 tablespoons = 30 mL
$^1\!/_4$ cup = 60 mL
$^1\!/_3$ cup = 75 mL
$^1\!/_2$ cup = 125 mL
$^2\!/_3$ cup = 150 mL
$^3\!/_4$ cup = 175 mL
1 cup = 250 mL
2 cups = 1 pint = 500 mL
3 cups = 750 mL
4 cups = 1 quart = 1 L

VOLUME MEASUREMENTS (fluid)

1 fluid ounce (2 tablespoons) = 30 mL
4 fluid ounces ($^1\!/_2$ cup) = 125 mL
8 fluid ounces (1 cup) = 250 mL
12 fluid ounces (1$^1\!/_2$ cups) = 375 mL
16 fluid ounces (2 cups) = 500 mL

WEIGHTS (mass)

$^1\!/_2$ ounce = 15 g
1 ounce = 30 g
3 ounces = 90 g
4 ounces = 120 g
8 ounces = 225 g
10 ounces = 285 g
12 ounces = 360 g
16 ounces = 1 pound = 450 g

DIMENSIONS

$^1\!/_{16}$ inch = 2 mm
$^1\!/_8$ inch = 3 mm
$^1\!/_4$ inch = 6 mm
$^1\!/_2$ inch = 1.5 cm
$^3\!/_4$ inch = 2 cm
1 inch = 2.5 cm

OVEN TEMPERATURES

250°F = 120°C
275°F = 140°C
300°F = 150°C
325°F = 160°C
350°F = 180°C
375°F = 190°C
400°F = 200°C
425°F = 220°C
450°F = 230°C

BAKING PAN AND DISH EQUIVALENTS

Utensil	Size in Inches	Size in Centimeters	Volume	Metric Volume
Baking or Cake Pan (square or rectangular)	8×8×2	20×20×5	8 cups	2 L
	9×9×2	23×23×5	10 cups	2.5 L
	13×9×2	33×23×5	12 cups	3 L
Loaf Pan	8$^1\!/_2$×4$^1\!/_2$×2$^1\!/_2$	21×11×6	6 cups	1.5 L
	9×9×3	23×13×7	8 cups	2 L
Round Layer Cake Pan	8×1$^1\!/_2$	20×4	4 cups	1 L
	9×1$^1\!/_2$	23×4	5 cups	1.25 L
Pie Plate	8×1$^1\!/_2$	20×4	4 cups	1 L
	9×1$^1\!/_2$	23×4	5 cups	1.25 L
Baking Dish or Casserole			1 quart/4 cups	1 L
			1$^1\!/_2$ quart/6 cups	1.5 L
			2 quart/8 cups	2 L
			3 quart/12 cups	3 L